SALT & PEPPER

you go together

by Jill Sweetman

Christian City Church

SALT & PEPPER: You Go Together
by Jill Sweetman

▣ Christian City Church

Published by c3 atlanta (Christian City Church)
1065 Walther Boulevard, Lawrenceville, Georgia 30043

ChristianCityChurch.com

Cover Art by Taylor Barriger
Editing and Interior Design by Lisa Beers
Printed by Instantpublisher.com

This book or parts thereof may not be reproduced in any form, stored in a retrieval system, or transmitted in any form by any means - electronic, mechanical, photocopy, recording, or otherwise - without prior written permission of the publisher, except as provided by US copyright law.

All scripture quotations, unless otherwise noted, are taken from *The Holy Bible, New King James Version.* Copyright © 1979, 1980, 1982 by Thomas Nelson, Inc. Broadman and Holman Publishers. Nashville, Tennessee.

Copyright 2005 Jill Sweetman. All rights reserved.
International Standard Book No (ISBN) 0-9753835-1-5

FOREWARD

As a young man, full of vision and faith for my ministry future, all I could think about was that if I wanted to be successful I needed a great wife. I was in full search mode in my late teens when I met Jill at a small group I was assisting in at the time. We became friends and got to know each other during the next eighteen months, and were married on March 30, 1985. I had gotten what I wanted, a beautiful girl, ministry minded, and dedicated to fulfilling my ministry dreams.

Little did I know that my pretext for marriage was floored. Over the next seven years we would go through all the ups and downs of early married life and then some. At near breaking point, when it seemed like I would loose everything, I finally came to a realization of what marriage really is. It certainly wasn't about me and my ministry dreams. I found out that God doesn't really need my ministry and the gifts He placed in my life. What He really wanted was for me to discover that Dean & Jill Sweetman were more important to Him than just Dean and his ministry. It was about us.

The context for me was ministry, but it could easily be any career or calling. Doctors, teachers, engineers all need to understand that it is always about that person you married before career pursuits. When I finally got this in perspective, our marriage began to work. It's still lots of hard work and commitment to the process, but I can honestly say that the last 13 years have been more that I could ever dream of, given the first seven. Having the right priorities in life and understanding the momentum they create changed everything for me. And guess what? All those early dreams and visions I had as a young man are coming to pass. Every single one of them. Not because I was all God had and was the only one who could do it. All our dreams are happening because I realized that they were all locked up inside my wife and our union together. All I had to do was be patient, love and serve her as Jesus has done for me, and allow my pride and selfishness to be replaced with love and servant hood.

You are going to love this book. It's real, authentic and penetrating. Open your heart and get ready to be challenged.

Dean Sweetman
Husband, Father, Minister

THANKS

There are many people who, without their existence, influence and input, this book could never have been conceived, written, and published.

Thank you Dean, for two incredible decades of learning and growing together in this process of marriage. The lessons we have learned, and still are learning everyday, shape my personality and character and help God to do His awesome work in me. I love you.

To our boys Jake and Barn, you light up my world and challenge me to be the woman, wife and mother that God intends.

My deep appreciation to Dr. Phil and Chris Pringle for your love, support, and wonderful example and impact on my life. Christian City Church Oxford Falls, with it's awesome staff and leadership, helped guide me through the early years of my marriage and provided the support I needed to stay committed to Dean and find God's voice when I needed to hear it the most.

Thanks also to our amazing church, Christian City Church Atlanta. You are our extended family, and the ongoing and unending support you give Dean and I is a blessing to us both.

I also want to acknowledge the talented Taylor Barriger who designed the wonderful cover for this book. And thanks to my editor, Lisa Beers, who is always able to know what I mean and works hard to make sure everyone else will also.

CONTENTS

Introduction *8*

One :: *What Is Marriage?* *11*
Two :: *Spiritual Intimacy* *19*
Three :: *Who We Are* *29*
Four :: *What Is Love?* *37*
Five :: *Communication* *43*
Six :: *Fulfilling Needs in Marriage* *53*
Seven :: *Conflict and Disagreement* *61*
Eight :: *Sex and Intimacy* *71*
Nine :: *Expectations* *77*
Ten :: *Goals and Visions* *83*
Eleven :: *Responsibility* *89*
Twelve :: *Money* *101*
Thirteen :: *Parents and In-Laws* *109*
Fourteen :: *When Crises Strike!* *119*

Sources *124*
About the author *127*

SALT & PEPPER

you go together

INTRODUCTION

It is 20 years since our wedding day, what have we accomplished over the years? We have had two children, experienced many financial ups and downs, a marriage breakdown and reconstruction, built a great friendship and financial security, and gained a lot more wisdom. Apart from this I have developed a real sense of fun and adventure, and a closeness to my husband that I never thought possible.

I love marriage and I love my husband and children. I love life. Has it been easy? I could never say that, but on the other side of disaster there has always been a type of victory. It has not always been the type I might have anticipated, but our fantastic God has always brought us through.

One of my goals is to stay married to my original partner, so I work towards this, aiming to understand and help my husband. Another goal is to raise children that love and serve God, love and serve in the church, and love people. My children are my legacy, what I leave behind, and so life is always a juggling act of shifting from one priority to another.

It is possible to build a great marriage in these times, despite all the pressures that society presents. We worship a God that created marriage and believes in it - and in us. Having a great marriage takes obedience to God's Word, faith, action, and flexibility. It is not God's intention that we experience failure in marriage.

Even after a marriage breakdown or infidelity, a marriage can still work. This is because there is such a thing as truth. Truth lies beyond facts. Truth is higher than facts, it is God. Facts are just our perception of the events and attitudes around us and in us. Truth lies beyond emotion.

Often we give up on something because of pain, or because another so-called "solution" feels better to us at the time. However, there is little future in jumping from one "feel good" solution to another.

God's Word is God's thoughts, prophecy, and vision for our lives. There is no better path for us to walk. Part of life lies in learning how to stand and live in the present instead of dwelling in the past or trying to run into the future. To look forward and envision what is to come is great, but to ignore the lessons of today is foolish.

Regarding partners, I really do not know whether there is a "mister" or "misses right" out there for any of us. I do know that there are plenty of "not-rights," particularly once we are in a marriage relationship. And I do know that we need to focus on making our present marriage work.

Many Christians believe in the covenant of marriage, but it is often misconstrued. I see many women living with an unfaithful husband and accepting this as their lot in life. I see women that recluse in their marriage, using the term "wife" as an excuse for doing nothing with their lives. We need to make sure that we continue to grow and move forward in our marriages while not allowing ourselves to come to a grinding halt.

I believe that there is so much more to marriage than just getting married. Even though we may not achieve what we expected to on our wedding day, marriage is extremely rewarding.

Believe and know that as we focus on our God we see only in part, and that His vision is bigger than ours - for our lives and our marriages.

It is normal to have days of discontentment, disillusion, frustration, and disappointment. There are days when you feel totally disconnected from your spouse. But there should be more days of fun, anticipation, and the shared fulfillment of dreams.

Marriage is one of the biggest commitments that you will ever make. Whether you are young or old, as long as you are flexible, teachable, and forgiving (both of self and others), you can have a wonderful marriage.

Marriage is full of adjustments and surprises. It is also full of opportunities to experience fulfillment and contentment.

Marriage, like anything of value, takes work and sacrifice. The rewards of that combined effort is amazingly edifying and rewarding.

CHAPTER ONE
What Is Marriage?

People marry for many different reasons. Some positive reasons can be companionship, love, or a belief that God wills us to marry. Some people decide on marriage based on issues such as fear of loneliness, a desire to leave home, to spite family, or because of a pregnancy.

Whatever our reasons for marrying, ultimately, we must realize that marriage is a contract and a covenant created by God. That fact, however, is not enough to guarantee that marriage will work. Nor is it enough to make couples desire to stay together.

In the early years of my marriage I took a lot for granted. According to my opinion, divorce was something that weak and non-committed people did. It was not for someone such as myself, and so it was a rude surprise when several years into my marriage I realized that I was staring at that scenario. I was dragged from my sheltered world into an ugly reality. I realized that not believing in something was not enough to prevent it from happening. I also realized that marriage required action, effort, and work. Love is an action word, not just an emotion.

We need to realize that God highly values marriage. Malachi 2:15-16 says,

> [15]But did He not make them one, Having a remnant of the Spirit? And why one? He seeks godly offspring. Therefore take heed to your spirit, And let none deal treacherously with the wife of his youth. [16]For the LORD God of Israel says That He hates divorce, For it covers one's garment with violence," Says the LORD of

hosts. *"Therefore take heed to your spirit, That you do not deal treacherously."*

And so if we really do value God's opinion and supernatural power, we will not only endeavor to make our marriages work, but will even allow God to have His way in our lives.

Knowing how strongly God feels regarding this covenant, we need to put a great amount of effort into our marriages. Sometimes despite a lack of warm and fuzzy feelings towards our spouse, we need to act out of the commitment and the promises that we made to each other before God.

That you are saved, attend church regularly, and get great teaching also does not guarantee a great marriage. Because you come from a great family or don't have fights does not guarantee success. Because you want your marriage to work is not even a guarantee.

This all sounds so negative, but many couples that have experienced a marriage breakdown or divorce know it to be true.

Yes, God hates divorce. Yes, God wants great marriages. He wants to bless us in our lives, and sometimes it seems that this could happen more easily in life as a single, or in a new marriage after divorce. But God's purpose for our lives is not about just being happy.

However, concerning marriage, the Bible also outlines that there should be companionship not war, and intimacy that involves openness and fun. It talks of sharing one another's lives, and a commitment to one another.

It also encourages us to use our gifts, talents, and ideas, and this does not always mean together. We have many great families in our church. At every level of service, even among the pastors, we often find that one partner is more involved in church life than the other. This is great, as each partner is running with their gifts and strengths, and yet supporting and encouraging the other at the same time.

Dean and I work in the same church but often spend time apart.

What Is Marriage?

We both love sports, but he plays golf and I play tennis. We have tried playing sports together, but for the sake of our marriage, we have found it better to play different sports. We are proud of each other, and talk of each other's accomplishments as though we were playing on a world circuit. However, we would not make it through one match if we played together.

We work on developing ourselves independently, but we spend time together to build our marriage. If we are to build a marriage, each individual needs to build him or herself also.

And so what is a marriage?

It is a covenant, and this means that two people are committed to the relationship, and to protecting each other and the sanctity and privacy of the marriage. It is two people sharing their lives, but not becoming so enmeshed in each other that they lose all sense of their own identity. It is two people that plan together for now, and for the future, so that their paths intertwine and not separate. It is two people that endeavor to look out for the happiness and contentment of each other. It is two people who realize that ultimately they can make their own plans, but have the grace and flexibility to allow the Lord to shape them.

What Goes Wrong?

Few realize that when we enter a marriage relationship, we bring not only our hopes and plans for the future, but the baggage from our past. We are like pioneers in a new land. The territory is unfamiliar but we are hopeful for the future.

Often we view a successful person as one who never encounters problems; the successful family is so together that they hardly raise a voice at each other. We carry a "Brady Bunch" image in our minds. A difficult problem for the family is Greg breaking an arm at football, or Jan struggling with being a middle child. It amazes me that Mr. and Mrs. Brady breezed through blending their two families together.

But the successful person is the one that does not hold onto hopeful but unrealistic expectations and perceptions, but rather realizes that difficult days will come and can be overcome. Difficult times are in the future that is unknown to us. To get victory there has to be trial.

So as much as we bring hope into our marriages, we also bring difficulty. These two things constantly accompany us, and work hand in hand building our marriages - if we realize that problems are a normal part of life.

Mark 2:17 says,

When Jesus heard it, He said to them, "Those who are well have no need of a physician, but those who are sick. I did not come to call the righteous, but sinners, to repentance."

The above scripture points out that we are imperfect. We grate against one another with attitudes and opinions, and so create intense feelings. What is important is the way we handle these feelings.

As we strive for intimacy in our marriage, our partner's imperfections are going to become very apparent to us. The temptation will be to want to remove those imperfections without paying attention to our own. We need to ask ourselves what we are doing to create disharmony rather than what the other is doing. Through prayer, repentance, and faith, we are responsible to examine our own imperfections.

Predominantly our ideas and values reflect what we have been taught by our families, tradition, or culture, and therefore our ideas and values may not necessarily reflect God's views. With this in mind, even though many of us go to premarital teaching, we still act out of habit. We act out of need, insecurity, and wants. We need to listen to one another and be willing to change for the sake of the relationship.

I remember sitting in our premarital sessions as 19 and 21 year-olds and asking a pastor if our marriage would be hard work. He gave the honest answer of yes. That was not reassuring.

Even though we knew of all the Biblical terms - leaving your father and mother, cleaving, and oneness in marriage - Dean and I brought so much baggage into our marriage that all that Biblical knowledge was fairly useless. And we are not so very different from most other married couples today.

We so wanted a great marriage, so wanted to be great Christian examples, and so wanted to be respected. Yet there we were 7 years later, separated, one step from divorce. Most thought that the Sweetman marriage was over.

Dean had been a house church leader and youth pastor. I had run a women's group, and helped start the church elementary school. Dean and I both had loving and caring families, and we were well-educated people. We were always in church and had a lot of friends. We were hard workers and high achievers.

But there we were. Our full-time ministry was gone, our marriage was a mess, our dreams were smashed and our hearts devastated.

We were attending church, feeling like we were the talk of the church. But it was actually the act of staying under our church covering as discussed in Ephesians 5 that helped mend our marriage.

For us, there were several reasons that caused our marriage to disintegrate. I think I knew from the start of our relationship that we had some major baggage, which led to that question to my pastor at premarital sessions.

When people say that they had no idea that their marriage was in trouble, it can be true. I always knew that we had problems, but because no one else acknowledged this, I did not think anything crucial was wrong. I thought our struggles were like everyone else's. Our problems were not very obvious to those outside of the walls of our home.

I was used to dissatisfaction and frustration, lack of communication, and lack of intimacy. It was all part of my past.

But that did not mean that I liked it, and it accumulated as anger... toward Dean and the children.

And so I knew that we had problems, but just continued coping with the daily tasks of life. When moving house repeatedly, trying to get financially established, trying to get going in ministry, helping in church, and raising children, it is difficult to sit back and realize the need for help. This is not a rare situation.

Dean, as is the cast with most young guys, was unwilling to admit that we needed help. My one attempt at asking for advice failed miserably. I approached a single female pastor!

Dean was an only child, and young and zealous male, and was more interested in ministry than marriage. He had no idea how to communicate with or care for a young wife and children. In his mind, a minister was supposed to have a wife, but beyond that thought nothing really computed.

As we progressed in ministry, and he traveled overseas, my existence seemed more of a hindrance than help. When traveling as a young evangelist whose funds were short, I seemed unimportant. He was clueless in ways to include me, particularly since we thought about things so differently. Him always being so positive and me so negative!

Many assume on their marriage day that the mission has been completed. Each has found someone that helps them feel better, and so the goal is accomplished. Few realize that during the first years of marriage you are often just getting to know the other!

On that day of vows before God and others, whether we realize it or not, we are promising to look after, and give to, one another. Even to the point of giving up our "must haves" for the other, rather than having our own way. Submission is mutual. The husband is to lead as a Christ-like figure. This is not about power or control, but rather him giving up his own agenda for his wife. It means assuming responsibility for the health and development of the marriage. The wife chooses to love and respect her husband. Marriage is the commencement of a whole new life.

What Is Marriage?

:: *Focus Point* ::

What are your thoughts on the following...

What will you receive out of marriage that you would not receive by remaining single?

What are your reasons for marrying?

As your marriage progresses, you will learn new things about each other. Some of these things will be easy to accept or understand, while others may not be. You need to realize from the beginning that your partner is neither perfect nor able to fulfill all your wants and needs. Therefore, you cannot focus on the weaknesses or inadequacies of your partner; but rather focus on their strengths and on God. By developing your relationship with God, your needs are met in their entirety. You must keep an attitude of serving your partner without always expecting something in return. It is also necessary to realize that it is not your responsibility to change your partner, only yourself.

Read Matthew 7:1-5: **¹"Judge not, that you be not judged. ²For with what judgment you judge, you will be judged; and with the measure you use, it will be measured back to you. ³And why do you look at the speck in your brother's eye, but do not consider the plank in your own eye? ⁴Or how can you say to your brother, 'Let me remove the speck from your eye'; and look, a plank is in your own eye? ⁵Hypocrite! First remove the plank from your own eye, and then you will see clearly to remove the speck from your brother's eye."**

How can you apply this to your marriage?

CHAPTER TWO
Spiritual Intimacy

We hear so much about unhappy marriages because one partner is a believer and the other is not. Conflict also occurs in a marriage of two believers where one wants to go forward in God but the other does not share this desire. They are happy to have salvation, but beyond this they have little passion to serve God.

Originally this chapter was placed at the end of this book, but upon its completion I realized its importance and therefore it leapt many pages forward. Unless there is an understanding of this topic, many couples live as if in a vacuum concerning their spiritual lives and that of their partner.

That both partners call themselves Christians is just not enough to have a spiritually fulfilling marriage. In the luster of a new relationship we often feel that we can change the other person. In fact, due to these feelings, we often feel that we would do anything for the other. But as time passes we see that these feelings and motivations fade.

This is where we need to go back to our Christian basics, that love is a commitment. As we move toward this we change, and the feelings resurface again. Why does this happen? Because our relationship with Christ includes the spiritual dimension and a currency of faith. We base our relationship on truth rather than the facts that may not appear too appealing at the time.

What is spiritual intimacy? I believe it to be the most important component of a marriage, where both partners have a desire to be close to God and follow His direction for their lives. Any other way leads to disillusionment and dissatisfaction as one partner (or both) seek fulfillment in other ways.

Spiritual intimacy between couples is not always comfortable and immediate, and can take time to develop. As you let this happen between you, you will find that God will use you as a couple, and your hearts and decisions will become more similar rather than different.

Spiritual growth comes when both partners submit to Christ, rather than one competing with the other to have their own way. God favors none over another; he is equally interested in both partners and their marriage.

I believe that in a Christian marriage both partners need similar beliefs. When there are differences, spiritual growth together becomes very difficult. For example, one may believe in the use of spiritual gifts while the other does not. It becomes difficult to share God's revelations where this type of difference exists. I also believe that a couple needs to enjoy a similar style of worship, as your church home is where you will receive a majority of your spiritual food and friendships. Do not think that you will get married and change your partner's beliefs! They probably are thinking exactly the same thing about you.

To develop spiritual intimacy it is important to know some background about one another. What were you taught by your parents concerning God, church, and the Bible? To be flexible and open in this area is so important since holding to traditions rather than pursuing our own knowledge is foolish.

To stay in a church because granny is "resting" in the graveyard, or because it has pretty stained glass windows, is irrelevant. It is not that these things are wrong, but they are just not valid reasons to commit to a church. Church is not something that we go to, but it is something that we are. We are a part of a body - the local church.

My parents encouraged my church attendance, but to rest only on this foundation stunts our growth. I had, and have, a responsibility to find answers for myself if I am to grow in my relationship with Christ. There is an even greater need in this area when we have children.

Many believe that spirituality has to do with the number of hours that one prays each day, or that a truly spiritual person spends much time studying the Bible. Most of us do need to discipline ourselves to spend time with God. If we sincerely believe that God is the first priority in our lives, we will discipline ourselves to get to know Him more.

Deuteronomy 6:5 says,

You shall love the LORD your God with all your heart, with all your soul, and with all your strength.

However, this is not easy in a world where most people work, sleep, pay bills, and raise families, all apart from attending church. We will come to a grinding halt however, unless we do spend time with our Creator. He understands us better than anyone, and so to go to the source of the one that made us makes total sense.

How do we become more spiritual? We do need to read and pray. Every one of us is unique. Some of us find it easy to pray or read for hours while others of us don't. Some of us find it easier to pray with worship music playing while others of us find it distracting. Others of us are morning people while some love the evening to spend time with God.

I myself find it difficult to pray if my bed is unmade or if dirty dishes are still in the sink. That is my melancholy nature, not that I can always use that as an excuse. I have to shut my eyes at times and not see the mess so that I do spend time with God.

I quite enjoy studying, and so I have acquired different Bible translations and books over the years to enhance my reading. And because I enjoy variety, I change the room in which I pray. I listen to teaching tapes and take notes because I lose concentration. This is not something that I naturally do, but I have put effort in over the years and now it is a habit.

Some of us enjoy the company of others in our spiritual pursuit, while others of us are loners. Some love to serve in the House of God, and this enhances their sense of spirituality, while others struggle to get involved in any way at all.

A couple of years ago, Dean and I wanted to provide one of our fantastic deacon couples with a night off. We held an appreciation night and told them to just show up and relax. This was so uncomfortable for them, as their love for God and spirituality is so connected with serving. It does not tire them, but rather invigorates them. There are so many pathways that enhance our connection with God, and we need to take care that we realize this, for one another's sake.

Just as a marriage requires action beyond communication, and learning about one another, so does our relationship with God. We read, study, and pray, but we also put this into effect. The Bible calls it fruit. The outer workings of our relationship with our Creator should produce fruit.

Galatians 5:22-26 says,

> **22But the fruit of the Spirit is love, joy, peace, longsuffering, kindness, goodness, faithfulness, 23gentleness, self-control. Against such there is no law. 24And those who are Christ's have crucified the flesh with its passions and desires. 25If we live in the Spirit, let us also walk in the Spirit. 26Let us not become conceited, provoking one another, envying one another.**

When we see the above qualities that are the outer workings of our relationship with God, we can understand that any relationship is going to benefit. We should practice this in our marriage, in our family, in our church, friendships, and even in our workplaces.

The point is that our spirituality is not measured by appearance, our works, or how much of the Bible we know from memory. It has nothing to do with church attire, a certain style of clothing, or how many church meetings or conferences we attend. Many confuse spirituality with the amount of the Bible we know. We are deluded by a thought that if we have enough knowledge we will feel better and be more spiritual.

Our lives are not measured by knowledge, but by fruit and faith. This means that the "look" of our spirituality will appear in our actions and attitudes.

Ephesians 2:8-9 says,

⁸For by grace you have been saved through faith, and that not of yourselves; it is the gift of God, ⁹not of works, lest anyone should boast.

And so if we have a whole lot of Bible knowledge but are not producing fruit, or if we know scripture but are not loving our family and friends, we need to make adjustments. The spiritual person is a doer of the Word.

John 1:1 says,

¹In the beginning was the Word, and the Word was with God, and the Word was God.

Spirituality should make us more relatable and not weird. It is not being a great speaker or performing miracles or using any talent. These are simply gifts given to each of us. As we mature in our spirituality, we should actually become more relatable and more appealing to others. People will want to be around us and know us.

If we are growing spiritually we are endeavoring to live the Bible, and be "doers of the Word." Not necessarily performing the customs of Biblical times such as braiding our hair, washing each others feet, and wearing head coverings, but rather putting on the character of God. These customs suited the culture of the time, but have no purpose today. For example, there was no asphalt on the roads in Jesus' day, and so the dust made necessary foot washings on a regular basis. Rather than offering to wash someone's feet though, the gift of a pedicure or manicure is far more relevant today.

We grow in time by prayer, reading, and being a part of a church body. The latter is often shunned, but helps a marriage by holding us accountable. Church on television cannot substitute. There are no real relationships or accountability. By mixing with other people, we see our strengths and weaknesses.

I find that people talk a lot about offense, that the church has offended them in some ways. Over the years, I have found it invaluable to be offended, both by my husband and by church. It is not that I like it, but offense is a way to learn of the areas which I need to change. Why? Because I can sit, get hurt, and hold a grudge, or I can choose to look at myself and see where I need to adjust. We always come back to that principle that our lives are our own responsibility. God does not need me to judge and change another. Church is just like a marriage. We get to see the reality of each other.

In a crisis, rather than meditating on the fact that our "dirty laundry" is being uncovered (which is usually humiliating and a hit to the ego), we should realize that there is no better place for this to be dealt with. The church is our covering, not just for ourselves, but for the entire family.

And so rather than disappearing from the church in shame because our marriage is collapsing, then showing up a couple of years later with a new marriage partner, we should walk through our crisis with the church and in church, under the covering that God has provided, allowing believers to speak faith into us.

This does not mean that every church member needs to know, or that they will all say what we need to hear. No, our lives never unfold in this manner. But the church is the covering beyond our husbands that was put in place by God. A truly spiritual person recognizes that Ephesians 5 is showing us that as a man is head of a wife, so a church provides headship and covering for a family.

In times of ease, through worship and teaching, we tank up for the difficult times. Don't wait for tough times to hit to be fed.

In pursuit of spiritual intimacy, there are other things that one partner can discuss with the other, such as conversion and water baptism. Perhaps they were momentous occasions or perhaps not. Perhaps you believe in the baptism of the Holy Spirit as a second experience. This can also be discussed.

Many of us experienced occasions growing up that really impacted our lives spiritually. Perhaps it was someone that impacted our life. It could have been a family member or a great friend. We get to know and understand each other as we share our thoughts and lives.

Dean often talked respectfully of an acquaintance who I thought was a really odd person, and so I questioned his honor, only to find out that this person was very instrumental in Dean's conversion. My opinion immediately changed.

Many of us carry memories of our first experiences of church. I knew only of one type of church for eighteen years and for some reason felt that all other churches were wrong, even though I was not taught this!

. . . .

:: *Focus Point* ::

How did you feel about the first church that you regularly attended? As a child or teen growing up, was there anything that really mystified you about God?

For years I thought that the Holy Spirit was an invisible mist that lingered only in the church building. I also thought that God was against wealth and anything to do with fashion. And so I felt tremendously guilty spending money on myself and would always try to explain away any new attire or house furnishing. I think that I must have believed that Jesus ministered only in one ratty old toga with little to eat and no place to sleep. As I explored the scriptures, I found that His life was an entirely different scenario.

What queries do you have concerning God or the church? Do you feel that anyone has really let you down spiritually?

Before we form opinions, it is wise to check that we have an open mind and are constantly forgiving. Some of the funniest scenarios in church life happen when someone expresses forgiveness to you over an episode that happened years ago and you were clueless as to having caused offense. It leaves one with strange emotions.

How do you enjoy spending time with God? Do you enjoy reading the Word, praying, spending time alone with God, or fellowshipping with other believers? Do you really enjoy praise and worship, serving in church, or are you an avid studier?

Bill Hybels in his book Courageous Leadership *has great information that helps us discover ways in which we find fulfillment in our relationship with Christ. It is enlightening and worth reading.*

There are numerous ways in which we can connect with our Father. Perhaps you have not discovered your pathway yet. Try some of the ideas previously listed, but no matter what, it is probably going to be different from your partner's. We need to respect this about one another, not trying to transform them into us.

Dean enthusiastically attends meeting after meeting while I slowly fade and grind to a halt. I love church but I need solitary time. I also love music. It inspires and encourages me. As I have said, I enjoy reading, but I have to discipline myself to read my Bible and supplement the diet with a variety of translations and reading materials.

We do not think of one of us as less spiritual than the other, but realize that each of us connects deeply with God in different ways.

How do you see yourself serving Christ? How does your

Spiritual Intimacy

partner feel about this?

Many couples desire to do something in church together but this sometimes does not happen immediately or at all. Sometimes one strongly desires to work in ministry while the other has no such plans. A person may see himself or herself in the workforce and never serving in church beyond attendance and giving financially.

Talk your plans through with each other but realize that plans can change. Realize that it is not wise to plan to change your partner. Do not marry thinking that you will change their minds after the marriage. Rather, ascertain that all big endeavors pursued should only be commenced with full approval of your partner. People grow apart because one or the other undertakes a venture without the agreement of the other. Your goal is to love and support each other through endeavors, both hardships and successes, "til death do us part."

. . . .

CHAPTER THREE

Who We Are

People are drawn to each other because of their similarities as well as their differences. The very things you first cherish in each other can become the very things you later dislike.

There is so much in our pasts that contribute to who we are, whether we like it or not. Our childhood, friends, schooling, financial backgrounds, hobbies, talents, achievements, and home life all affect our reactions, personality, and decision-making processes.

When we met, Dean was the outgoing worship leader, or "star," on the stage at church, while I was a quiet and shy church member with big dreams. I so loved Dean's confidence, aspirations, and vision. These were some of his traits that first made me fall in love with him. However as years progressed, I became frustrated as I longed for some security and a fulfillment of those dreams that kept alluding us.

In six years of marriage, and with two baby boys born seventeen months apart, we moved more than ten times. We lived with parents and we lived in a bus. We spent several years sleeping in an unfinished attic, then moved into a house (in the middle of winter) that was missing half its outer wall. My admiration for Dean's great vision was wearing thin as we seemed to be on a continuous downward spiral.

Dean is an only child. He was not used to much conversation after a day of work. I am the middle daughter of three girls and knew very little about boys. While Dean had to adjust to a talkative wife, I had to adjust to having less conversation than in my childhood home as part of a family of five.

Dean loves to socialize. On the very first day home after our honeymoon, he came back from church with about ten extra people. To him, the explanation of "you don't mind babe?" was more than adequate for his new wife who loved order and peace. My intention was to cuddle on the couch all afternoon watching television, just him and I.

We have to learn how to respect and handle our similarities and differences.

Putting The Past Into Perspective

We also have to deal with fears, embarrassment, rejection, or disappointment from our pasts. For example, I was never destined for success in track, so year after year I found myself crossing the finishing line at the very end of the pack. Even now, I still detest running!

But I always know that I was designed and created by an almighty and powerful God. His plan for me is not to be devastatingly wounded in my past. I learned to look beyond my past to my loving Father, our Creator. We can all look to a great future, seeing our past and present as preparation for that future. Our failures should be looked at simply as lessons learned. Wounds should not shape our lives to our detriment, but rather teach and prepare us for that which lies ahead.

Our marriage breakdown equipped us for a better marriage. There was shock and hurt, but as we endeavored to keep to our commitment we were restored. In marriage, we not only commit to one another, but also to God. This is very powerful.

Our Responsibility For Change

Each one of us has been uniquely made. God designed every person individually and we should keep this in mind as we discover our similarities and learn to embrace differences.

Psalm 139:14-16 says,

^{14}I will praise You, for I am fearfully and wonderfully made; Marvelous are Your works,

And that my soul knows very well.
¹⁵My frame was not hidden from You,
When I was made in secret,
And skillfully wrought in the lowest parts of the earth.
¹⁶Your eyes saw my substance, being yet unformed.
And in Your book they all were written,
The days fashioned for me,
When as yet there were none of them.

While it is true that some things such as habits or daily routines can be changed, it is also true that others things cannot. Age, race, and background cannot be changed and must be carefully considered before embarking on a marriage.

Sometimes we view relationships in the way we might regard a piece of furniture. It gets old, worn, and unappealing so we discard it for a newer item. There is nothing wrong with dealing with things in this manner, but it should not be how we handle our marriage and relationships.

The Bible instructs us to allow ourselves to be changed so that we become more like God. When we annoy or frustrate each other we need to look at what we can change within ourselves rather than dwell upon the other's habits. As we continue to look to God we are reminded that not only did we commit ourselves to another person in marriage, we committed to a promise before God. We can change.

As a young married couple, Dean and I eventually looked at our crazy life full of house moves. We both realized that we needed to make some adjustments. I was to change myself and Dean was to change himself, we were not to embark on a mission of changing each other. We are only responsible for changing ourselves.

For many years I battled poor self-esteem. I fought with thoughts of failure regarding myself to the degree that I would not recognize any success that I achieved. If I received a compliment I would refute it. This frustrated Dean to no end. I decided to change when I realized that this affected my love - not only my love for myself, but for those around me and for God. I did not want this problem to affect my marriage and children.

I took great comfort in Psalm 139, which made me realize that before I experienced anything on this earth, God had wonderfully and skillfully created me. It is also comforting to know that I am a redeemed person, as is any believer. Galatians 3:14 says,

14*He redeemed us in order that the blessing given to Abraham might come to the Gentiles through Christ Jesus, so that by faith we might receive the promise of the Spirit.*

God's Word is a supernatural tool that we need to allow to penetrate our hearts. God's House, the local church, is not a building to attend, but something we need to belong to and attach ourselves to. Ephesians 5 teaches us so clearly that Jesus is the head of the church ("the releaser of life") and we are the body. Jesus gives us life through the local church. As we are taught and as we read our Bibles, we need to allow our minds to be renewed. We should not just memorize the Bible, but allow it to make us more Christ like. Choose to change!

Romans 12:2 says,

2*And do not be conformed to this world, but be transformed by the renewing of your mind, that you may prove what is that good and acceptable and perfect will of God.*

Differences in our personalities and backgrounds can also cause hurt and confusion. As we work through and communicate about these areas in our marriage, we can eventually appreciate the differences that cause conflict. You did not marry the wrong partner after all! It is not our job to remake our partners, but to discover and value their differences. We complement one another and can enjoy life together. It is best to examine yourself and ask, "What is it that

I am misunderstanding, or that I need to change within myself?"

Looking at it in another light, it is rather arrogant to think that we have the right to change someone else. God has given our partner to us as a gift and the realization of this is very humbling. He has given one of His creation to us. As we yield to one another and view our partner as a gift, God changes both of us.

If we allow God to continually change each of us, and not try to make our partners be what we think they should be, our marriages will prosper. God does not want marriages to deteriorate and fail - He desires success!

Marriage is one of the greatest opportunities we have to put all of this into practice. As a couple, each of us sees our partner in a way that others will not. This is not an excuse to break a commitment. It is an opportunity to know someone in a way that no one else, apart from God, has the privilege. It is an opportunity to grow in character. Hold on to God's perspective rather than our tainted one. Each of us "is fearfully and wonderfully made. Marvelous are your works."

Security and Contentment

God knows the life that we have yet to live, and has created for us a wonderful future in Him. Jeremiah 29:11 says,

> *11For I know the thoughts that I think toward you, says the LORD, thoughts of peace and not of evil, to give you a future and a hope.*

We don't feel this every hour and day of our lives, but it is what God has promised each of us as we press into His Word and teachings. I remember the pain and despair of difficult times, but I also remember that in moments of dwelling on God there was a true sense of peace and safety for my future. We should hold onto this when our lives are not progressing according to our plans.

It is not right or fair to depend on your spouse for total security, in the present or for the future. We were created for a relationship with God, and so each of us will only feel replenished when we rely on our Maker.

I have met many people that walked away from a marriage, only to find later that what they left was actually what they wanted. When we only serve our own needs we build a lonely life, but when we look to fill the needs of another we find contentment. This is because God created us for relationship. In Genesis we see God speaking out the creation, the making of mankind. Early in His creation God says, "It is not good that man be alone."

As we look around we see the awesome diversity of people that God created. It is interesting that often the things that once drew us together can start to cause friction in a marriage. But as we consider one another, and are honest and gentle with our words, we will find a growing appreciation of one another.

Psalm 19:14 says,

[14]Let the words of my mouth and the meditation of my heart Be acceptable in Your sight, O LORD, my strength and my Redeemer.

Once you are married, know that you are just starting the journey. You are still discovering the uniqueness of the other person.

Marriage is more of a verb than a noun, more of an action than an event. It is achieved by moving through life chapter by chapter. It is never finished, so we need to continually put on love and be transformed by the renewing of our mind.

:: Focus Point ::

How did you feel about yourself in your childhood and in your teen years?

Outline some of the differences between you and your partner.

How will these affect your marriage?

CHAPTER FOUR

What Is Love?

I remember walking down the aisle on my wedding day and wondering what on earth I was doing! Was I really getting married? I had been through several relationships - in love, out of love, is this love, what is love?

Society today promotes love as that warm and exciting feeling that quickly leads to jumping into bed with one another. Even the gender of your partner is hardly relevant in our culture today.

To build our marriages on this feeling sets us up for failure, since it will come and go in the life of any relationship. And then too, it is easy to become so involved in the preparation for the marriage ceremony that the years following the event seem forgotten.

If we realize that love is not the basis for marriage, but the outcome of a successful marriage, it relieves a lot of pressure. As we set our minds to give and cultivate love, we can create the rosy, tingly emotion that we crave.

The book of Proverbs offers some incredible teachings on relationships of every kind, from friendships to marriage. It challenges and inspires us in all walks of life. It instructs us on everyday reactions and actions towards one another. It is a fantastic reminder of the ways in which we are to value one another.

One of the most valuable keys in marriage is this: the only person you are responsible to change is yourself, and this needs to be in the area of increasing your Godly character. If you actively allow the Holy Spirit to change you into the image of Christ, you will be less likely to notice your partner's shortcomings. Your partner will however benefit from the changes that are occurring within you.

If your marriage is to succeed, it will take more than just hoping for the best. Simply knowing what God feels about marriage alone will not hold a marriage together. The participants must press through their upbringings, traditions, and mindsets to truly believe that marriage can last a lifetime. Life has a way of helping you discover any weaknesses in yourself, your belief system, or faith in general. When the tough times come, you will be presented with many opportunities to quit. Yet these pressure-filled times can be seized as events that lead toward growth, individually and as a couple. Or they can seemingly provide you with valid reasons for walking out of the relationship.

During these difficult times excuses abound, however one thing remains constant - God is into marriage regardless of one's reasons for getting married. God can make a marriage something great and lasting whether it was born out of fear, rebellion, a pregnancy or His will. Obtaining this kind of marriage will take a commitment to God and each other.

Look at the following passages and consider the concepts presented.

Giving Not Getting :: Philippians 2:3-5
³Let nothing be done through selfish ambition or conceit, but in lowliness of mind let each esteem others better than himself. ⁴Let each of you look out not only for his own interests, but also for the interests of others. ⁵Let this mind be in you which was also in Christ Jesus,

Loving God Above All :: Matthew 22:37-39
³⁷Jesus said to him, "You shall love the LORD your God with all your heart, with all your soul, and with all your mind. ³⁸This is the first and great commandment. ³⁹And the second is like it: You shall love your neighbor as yourself."

Qualities of Love :: 1 Corinthians 13:4-7
⁴Love suffers long and is kind; love does not envy; love does not parade itself, is not puffed up; ⁵does not behave rudely, does not seek its own, is not provoked, thinks

no evil; ⁶*does not rejoice in iniquity, but rejoices in the truth;* ⁷*bears all things, believes all things, hopes all things, endures all things.*

Ephesians 4:2
²*with all lowliness and gentleness, with longsuffering, bearing with one another in love,*

The Role of each Partner :: Ephesians 5:22-25
²²*Wives, submit to your own husbands, as to the Lord.* ²³*For the husband is head of the wife, as also Christ is head of the church; and He is the Savior of the body.* ²⁴*Therefore, just as the church is subject to Christ, so let the wives be to their own husbands in everything.* ²⁵*Husbands, love your wives, just as Christ also loved the church and gave Himself for her.*

All of the above scriptures cause us to acknowledge another's needs before that of our own. Our priority should be that we recognize the value of our spouse as another human being, and want to bless them and see them grow as a Christian.

In my early years of my marriage I struggled to value Dean because of my own poor esteem. It is difficult to value another when we do not value ourselves. It is also difficult to be humble when we continually battle thoughts of insignificance and insecurity. We continually try to validate our worth.

A humble heart releases consideration, care, and concern that respects another's life. A poor self-esteem is not indicative of a humble person. Often a person of poor self worth is very proud. They are consumed by their own needs and therefore cannot cope with the needs or demands of another. People in this state often marry hoping that the other will validate their existence, but this is an impossible task. No matter how much one tries to praise the other, they find that the need is never met.

If anyone struggles with a lack of love for them selves, meditate on scriptures that fill you with revelation regarding God's thoughts and plans for you. "Meditate" means to ponder, or to speak over and over. As we do this with scripture, we begin to see ourselves as God does. A poor self-image warps our love and care of others.

Remember that our human love will be inconsistent and imperfect, so we need to allow our marriages to be undergirded by His divine love.

Types of Love

Most people totally rely on their feelings as the determining factor on choosing a mate. In actuality there are different types of love. If you desire to keep love alive in your marriage and relationships, you will need to make a conscious effort to understand and apply each of these three types of love: eros, phylia and agape.

Eros is the romantic love, or sexual love, that seeks sensual expression. It is part of our biological makeup. In a good marriage a husband and wife love each other emotionally and erotically. It is far more than just two people achieving sexual satisfaction, but this will be discussed more in a later chapter.

Philial love is expressed through the friendship, companionship, cooperation, and communication within your relationship.

Agape is a love that reveals itself through selflessness. This love gives to others. This is the love that keeps on loving when it seems there is no more love to give or one seems unlovable. This love is based on a commitment; it does not just happen. It is a choice that goes beyond feelings.

If love is to thrive and continue, it will take operating in all these areas of love. Love begins to falter when one stops complimenting the other, or a couple fails to spend time together doing things both partners enjoy. Love is kept alive by a conscious effort to maintain it from both the partners.

After the initial sparks that attract you to your partner begin to fade, you will need to continue to share ideas, thoughts, and concerns (philia). You will need to physically show that you care (eros), and sometimes you will have to delay your wants and needs for gratification and put your partner first (agape). It is very important to remain each other's greatest support, and consider each other with respect and honor, making sure your words are edifying and encouraging.

Because all three types of love are interrelated, you will generally find that one type of love will be in the forefront more at certain times, while at other times another type of love will be more dominate. This is normal over time in a relationship when balance is seen in the overall picture.

In a marriage, love grows over years as each partner determines to share his life with the other partner. As already noted, the early years of marriage are really just a time of discovery about the other. They are the beginning of getting to know each other.

The most sure and true way to learn how to love your partner can be found by examining the love of Christ. His love, the example of the greatest love, is a gift. Christ demonstrates sacrificial love, unconditional love, sympathy, thoughtfulness, eternal love and so much more. Nowhere does He say "I will love you if..." When you find yourself in a time of not feeling a lot of love towards your partner, look more closely at the way Christ loves. Let Christ enable you during those times because of your commitment to Him. By being committed, the feelings will return and your partner will reap the benefits.

:: Focus Point ::
Put yourself in your partner's place and think of his likes and dislikes.

This is very important because when you marry, his/her hopes and dreams become important to you.

CHAPTER FIVE

Communication

"I know what I want to say but I do not know how to say it!"

This is heard so often between married couples, and unfortunately, many never learn how to effectively communicate. Other misunderstandings occur because we think we know what our partners are saying, but we miss the point because of our own filters and barriers.

It is said that 75% of what we orally communicate is ignored or forgotten. Yet probably the most important ingredient in a marriage is the ability to communicate. When we don't understand we need to ask more questions and gather more information until we have clarity.

Communication is the process of sharing yourself, verbally and non-verbally, in a way that the other person can accept and understand you. This means that listening is extremely important.

To make time to hear each other, to make sure that you are in an environment where you can listen to each other, is so important. Yes we need to make time to sit down, go to a coffee shop, or take a walk. Make it a priority. Get the children minded, cancel that golf game, let the other knows that they are the priority.

In a good relationship, the man and woman both realize that there is unity in love, but at the same time there is freedom of opinion for both individuals. Neither is swallowed up by the other, but each keeps his personality and identity. In a secure marriage, each can be honest about all types of feelings and can talk about their differences, airing even hostility and hurt. The intention is never to offend the other, but in their security with each other, they kiss and make up and have a great chance of growing old together.

Proverbs 21:11 says,

> *11 The wise man learns by listening; the simpleton can learn only by seeing scorners punished.*

James 1:19 says,

> *19 Let every man be quick to hear, slow to speak, and slow to anger.*

When we are really listening, we are not thinking about what we are going to say next. Listening is also a complete acceptance of what and how something is said. Often we do not accept a message due to a tone of voice, or because we do not like the message. We miss what is being shared.

Acceptance does not mean that we agree, but that we understand that what the other person is saying is something he feels. Real listening means that we should be able to repeat what is said to us and what we think the other was feeling.

If you are not sure what your partner is saying, ask more questions to gather more information and learn not to jump to conclusions.

Levels of Communication

There are different levels of communication, ranging from cliché or safe conversation with no real personal sharing, to emotional and personal communication where absolute honesty and openness occurs. The latter involves the risk of rejection, but it is vital if relationships are to grow. There will be times when this communication is not as it should be.

Close relationships usually fall into the latter category, and this is the level for which you are aiming with your relationship with God.

Cognitive or Emotional Communication

People tend to communicate either more on a cognitive

(thinking) level, or on an emotional level. The former usually tend to talk about facts, such as sports and occupations. They will feel more comfortable keeping the subject out of the emotional area and often have trouble being warm or supportive of their partners. The latter, however, communicate more on the emotional level and tire of facts. They desire to share feelings, especially with their partners. They speak to obtain emotional clarity and will strive for this. People from both communication "camps" are probably coming to your mind even as you are reading this.

If you move around the room at a gathering such as at a wedding reception or party, you will see examples of both types of communication. Some groups will be comfortably involved in factual conversations while others will find this trivial and will be attracted more to those who are drawn to deeper conversation, topics that involve more of an emotional input and sharing. It is important to point out though that no one is completely cognitive or emotional.

I was raised in a family of five and was the middle daughter of three sisters, each of us three years apart. And so, even though communication was not perfect, it was there. There was laughter and bickering in the midst of clothing and shoe swaps and diets. Mom and Dad both worked from the early years of our lives.

Meanwhile several suburbs away, Dean was an only child, also from a family where both parents worked. The closest thing he had to a sibling was a pet rabbit. He did not have to communicate closely often at all. Then we got married!

I spent the first few years of our marriage in assumption, assuming that Dean felt this or that. It frustrated me greatly that he would be the life of a party among friends, and then at home little would be expressed. Among friends he would not discuss anything of a personal nature, but at least he talked. He seemed to enjoy and respond to others' companionship so much more than to mine. I desperately craved emotional intimacy through one to one conversation. I was looking for emotional clarity.

Through yelling and nagging, I caused Dean to talk to me

SALT & PEPPER: *you go together*

even less. Proverbs 19:13 talks of "the contentions of a wife are a continual dripping." That was me! I was creating an unpleasant environment that squashed communication rather than inviting it. Great communication and intimacy rarely just happen. It is developed. It is something to which we give time and attention.

....
:: Focus Point ::

> Regarding cognitive and emotional communication, to which direction do you think that you are inclined? To which direction is your partner inclined?

....

The more emotionally inclined person is not less intelligent, but is more aware of his or her feelings. Therefore he is usually better able to communicate them. The cognitive person is just as sensitive, but does not usually express this. Since the cognitive person buries his feelings, he may find an emotional partner or child frustrating because he is not used to operating on this level.

In a marriage, both partners need to learn to understand each other. This takes time and patience. For some it will mean to look beyond the face shown them by the non-emotional partner. For those with the emotional partner, they must hear the message that is being conveyed apart from the emotions.

Nonverbal Communication

Consideration also needs to be given to nonverbal communication. People send messages, and each message has three parts: the content, the voice tone, and the nonverbal communication. Nonverbal communication is defined as the actions, body language and facial expressions of the speaker. Simply by changing one's tone of voice and nonverbal communication, the entire message can change. This is because tone of voice and nonverbal communication

Communication

(actions, body language and facial expressions) tend to hold more weight than the content of the message itself.

....
:: *Focus Point* ::

Consider your non-verbal cues.

How do you show affection to your partner with nonverbal cues? How does your partner?
....

One of the most important keys to effective communication is learning to keep a conversation open rather than shutting it down. We need to gather the whole story rather than assuming or supposing. The following can be detrimental to communication:

- Sarcasm or very dry humor.

- Emotionally loaded comments. For example, calling someone weak rather than gentle.

- Exaggeration of the real situation - "You never do what I ask!"

- Arguments that divert from the real situation - "You left the door open again" and "Well you didn't cut the grass last week."

Because none of the above encourages honesty, they should be avoided. The above stated qualities are more about trying to win an argument than promoting healthy and beneficial communication. All of the above usually result in wondering what the argument was about originally.

The following scriptures provide keys to good communication.

Consider the Biblical principle involved.

Power of Words :: Proverbs 15:4
⁴The tongue that brings healing is a tree of life,
but a deceitful tongue crushes the spirit.

Slow to Speak :: Proverbs 15:28
²⁸The heart of the righteous weighs its answers,
but the mouth of the wicked gushes evil.

Not Holding Grudges :: Proverbs 17:14
¹⁴Starting a quarrel is like breaching a dam;
so drop the matter before a dispute breaks out.

Listening :: Proverbs 18:13
¹³He who answers before listening -
that is his folly and his shame.

Not Nagging :: Proverbs 17:9
⁹He who covers over an offense promotes love,
but whoever repeats the matter separates close friends.

Speaking The Truth :: Ephesians 4:25-27
²⁵Therefore each of you must put off falsehood and speak truthfully to his neighbor, for we are all members of one body. ²⁶"In your anger do not sin": Do not let the sun go down while you are still angry, ²⁷and do not give the devil a foothold.

Being Understanding :: Ephesians 4:2
²Be completely humble and gentle; be patient, bearing with one another in love.

Not Accusing :: Galatians 6:1
¹Brothers, if someone is caught in a sin, you who are spiritual should restore him gently. But watch yourself,

or you also may be tempted.

Finally, the following are great keys that I have gathered over the years.

. . . .

If you want to see your partner's behavior change, focus on and change yourself rather than criticizing them. Change in them will come as a response to the changes that you make.

Focus on the behavior you desire rather than the problem. Notice that Paul's letters to the churches often used this format: praise, give the questionable behavior and a remedy, more praise. People are won by praise and are more likely to offer a positive response when they are not pushed towards a defensive position.

Learn to be able to say, "I'm sorry." It is easy to see another's faults but not so easy to admit your own. Being able to say these words is a key to successful living, and it allows the Holy Spirit access to our lives.

Be able to say " I love you" often. On your wedding day is not enough! This needs to be expressed through both words and actions. It is not good enough that you can show love only in front of others. It has to be in evidence at home.

Remember Philippians 2:3,

2"Do nothing from selfishness or empty conceit, but with humility of mind, let each of you regard one another as more than himself."

It is essential that you sit down and talk as a couple about your hurts and needs. Do this in a non-accusatory way making sure that you are ready to hear the other's comments as well as expressing your own.

. . . .

Communication

CHAPTER SIX
Fulfilling Needs In Marriage

Each one of us are motivated very strongly to have our needs met by another. When we marry, we promise to do our best to love our partners no matter what! "Til death do us part!"

Honestly though, we are very much hoping that our partner will be able to meet our needs. How often do we hear the following statements: "My needs are not being met," or "she does not understand or support me." Another typical statement heard is, "There's always been a gap between us."

With this in mind, it is important for a person to specifically define their needs and then to let their partner know how to meet those needs. It is not enough to assume that they are going to know what you want. Your feelings, desires, and insecurities should be communicated and understood by one another. This may not seem too romantic at first, but as time goes by and you get to know one another more, less talking and explaining will be needed.

As everyone is human and imperfect, neither partner will be able to completely fulfill the other's needs. If you expect unreasonable things, you will be disappointed and frustrated. As believers, we have to take responsibility for ourselves and our actions, and forgive our partner's shortcomings.

While we seek to fulfill our partner's needs, we will make mistakes along the way. We need to be ready to be renewed in our minds every day for the rest of our lives, as the Bible says in Romans 12:2,

²And do not be conformed to this world, but be

transformed by the renewing of your mind, that you may prove what is that good and acceptable and perfect will of God.

:: Focus Point ::

Consider the three areas listed and write down some of your needs. Discuss how you expect your partner to fulfill these needs.

- Physical
- Emotional
- Spiritual

There are also social and intellectual needs. Everyone has the same basic needs of food, shelter, and safety. Each person also has a need for love, a sense of belonging, to become the person he or she was created by God to be. Probably our greatest needs are to be needed and recognized.

Most husbands and wives fulfill the physiological and safety needs, such as having enough groceries and keeping the car running and the house safe. However, most start to fail at the higher level - that of a person's need for love, belonging, recognition and acceptance. This is why it is such a necessity to remember that it is God's desire for each of us to become the person that He created us to be. We each are full of so much potential.

A woman's need for esteem is primarily met by her husband, while a man's esteem is gained primarily in his work. Each of us needs to realize this, not just for ourselves, but for the sake of the other. A husband cannot pour his life into his career and then say that he is doing this for the family because his wife will end up feeling unimportant. His work is usually not as much about the needs of the family, but rather only giving him a sense of fulfillment. A balance has to be met. Of course a man must work as 2 Thessalonians 3:10 says, **"If anyone will not work, neither shall** *he eat."* But he must also realize that his wife's sense of value is strongly determined by his love and care for her.

We also need to be aware of our partner's personal needs. It is very important that we keep each others' needs and aspirations in mind, and that we are helping each other in achieving them. It is important that our partners feel our support. Otherwise we drift away from the other in a marriage.

For the sake of our marriages, each of us needs to reevaluate our personal goals so that our marriages and families do not suffer. As couples plan their future together, with each partner's desires and goals in mind, we move toward a fulfilling marriage.

....

:: Focus Point ::

How do you show your partner that they are important to you? Do they understand this?

....

As I have already discussed, there will be many times when the answer you seek cannot be found in your partner, and you have to accept this. Instead of relying on yourself or your partner to meet your needs, you need to rely on God's promises to us in the Bible that are exactly what you need. A Christian marriage is founded upon the faith that Christ is dwelling in each of us and therefore wants to help us overcome difficulties. He also helps us to live contentedly with our partner's weaknesses.

The following scriptures give valuable insight for this topic and so are well worth researching and meditating upon.

Ephesians 2:10
¹⁰For we are His workmanship, created in Christ Jesus for good works, which God prepared beforehand that we should walk in them.

Matthew 6:33-34
³³But seek first the kingdom of God and His righteousness, and all these things shall be added to you. ³⁴Therefore do not worry about tomorrow, for tomorrow will worry about its own things. Sufficient for the day is its own trouble.

Matthew 7:7-10
⁷Ask, and it will be given to you; seek, and you will find; knock, and it will be opened to you. ⁸For everyone who asks receives, and he who seeks finds, and to him who knocks it will be opened. ⁹Or what man is there among you who, if his son asks for bread, will give him a stone? ¹⁰Or if he asks for a fish, will he give him a serpent?

Romans 8:35-39
³⁵Who shall separate us from the love of Christ? Shall tribulation, or distress, or persecution, or famine, or nakedness, or peril, or sword? ³⁶As it is written: "For Your sake we are killed all day long; We are accounted as sheep for the slaughter." ³⁷Yet in all these things we are more than conquerors through Him who loved us. ³⁸For I am persuaded that neither death nor life, nor angels nor principalities nor powers, nor things present nor things to come, ³⁹nor height nor depth, nor any other created thing, shall be able to separate us from the love of God which is in Christ Jesus our Lord.

Jeremiah 29:11
¹¹For I know the thoughts that I think toward you, says the LORD, thoughts of peace and not of evil, to give you a future and a hope.

    This last scripture was instrumental in helping me realize that God actually had a unique plan for my life among the confusion of our early marital chaos. There was a reason for my existence beyond being Dean's wife.

Also as previously stated, self-image is one of the most important foundations of marriage. If your esteem is low, a strain will be placed upon your marriage. You may be marrying so that your spouse can give you a sense of meaning.

I believe that most of us battle with feelings of failure or insignificance at some point in our lives. I have come to view these two things as learning points or times in which we need to re-evaluate ourselves: who we are in God, and what we are doing with our lives. However, apart from this, we need to always encourage one another. Moreover, it is of special importance that we speak highly of our partner to others. Never put your partner down in public or ridicule them in a manner that makes them look or feel insufficient.

Most importantly, we each need to know of our worth in God, apart from the worth we get through others and our personal gifts and talents. That is why we need to be aware of the scriptures listed above.

Talents and gifts are fantastic and contribute to our sense of self-worth, but they are not us in our entirety. They do not enable a marriage to last. Often they can strain a marriage as one partner struggles to find their sense of significance when so much of the other's life revolves around a talent and its recognition.

. . . .

:: *Focus Point* ::

Our self-image tends to be built upon several things such as:

• The need for acceptance or belonging

• Status or the sense of personal importance

• Security or the sense of feeling safe

- Competence or the feeling of adequacy

As you look at these needs, think of the priority that they have in your life.

To what degree does your self-image depend on them? Does your partner agree with your answers?

....

There will be many times in your marriage when your partner does or does not fulfill your needs. All of the above are normal needs as long as you keep them in control and don't let them control you in a manner that drives you and your partner apart.

God assures us that we belong to Him. We are assured of competence and worthiness in Him and through Him. The Holy Spirit is our Comforter, our Guide, and in addition to that, our source of strength.

It is Jesus Christ in our lives that helps to fulfill our needs and our partners' needs. It is vital that we allow Him this position and not try to put our partner in His place.

Fulfilling Needs In Marriage

CHAPTER SEVEN
Conflict and Disagreement

Whether you like it or not, conflicts will happen in your marriage. Oftentimes couples believe that a great marriage is one with no conflict, but this is not true.

Conflict occurs when our desires differ. The problem lies not in our differences of opinion, but in our reactions. It is how a couple handles conflict and disagreements that determines the success or failure of their marriage.

After the novelty of the marriage is over, each partner's weaknesses begin to appear and disagreements surface. The weaknesses require adjustments, and we need to allow the Holy Spirit to turn the weaknesses into positive attributes.

Remember that the Christian life is all about living by a power beyond ourselves.

The security of a Christian marriage must be rooted in an ongoing and deepening relationship with Christ. If we continue to seek God and work to be more like Him, God accomplishes His purpose in our lives. God is into marriage. God's attitude to divorce is very clear in Malachi 2:16 when He says, *"I hate divorce."* His feelings toward divorce are also clear in other passages in the Bible. He prefers reconciliation to this act that creates lifelong separation between partners.

Many couples want their marriages to be a great witness for Christ but how do we establish this? It needs to be based on more than just being a couple.

As we develop any other relationship, our relationship with God needs time and energy as well. It is our relationship with Him that will grow our marriages. And so hearing from God, speaking to God, and knowing His book are very important. Make sure that you spend time reading your Bible and in prayer. Work out a time that fits your lifestyle, but realize also that if you are to grow, these things need to be a priority.

Some couples will want to do this together, while some will prefer their own private time with God. Both situations are fine when each partner shares with the other revelation, wisdom, and knowledge they acquire.

Dean and I have never enjoyed praying together but we regularly discuss the revelations that happen in our worlds. It is now a natural thing for us to do this. Other people pray and read their Bibles together. Go with that if it fits your lifestyle. However, make sure that you are telling each other your thoughts, ideas, and revelations also.

You also need to bring your relationship differences to God. We either ignore them, harbor them in our hearts, or bring them before God. We can discuss them with one another, but if Jesus is a healer then it makes sense to bring them before Him. Many couples continue to bring problems to each other only, expecting that the other will fix it or give in. We may win a few battles this way but usually it damages the marriage. Better to take it to a higher authority, the Lord God our Father.

On another note, not all differences need to be resolved to keep a marriage healthy. It is okay to have differing opinions over a period of time as long as they are not building up as resentment that will drive a marriage apart.

I envision being with Dean as my husband for the rest of our lives, and so I do not push to win all arguments. I give thought to how a difference is going to help my marriage. I consider what is most important, and know that some areas of disagreement are better forgotten.

In a new relationship it is important to discover how each other's families resolved conflict. Some families are very verbal while others refuse to talk about discrepancies. Dean and I knew of one couple that never fought. If tension arose, they would stop talking and pretend as if nothing happened. The marriage lasted for ten years. They are now divorced.

Often a person brings their family's method of dealing with conflict into their other relationships, not knowing of any other way to handle disagreement. Of course this is not always the best way. Both partners need to feel respected in their thoughts, emotions, and opinions. Sometimes we need to concede in an argument to preserve the relationship. Winning an argument usually means a loss in the growth of your marriage. In other words, you may win the fight but it has damaged your relationship.

....
:: Focus Point ::

We need to consider the following:

Do you find it hard to allow your partner to have a different opinion?

What opinions differ between you and your partner?

Which of these are you happy to leave unresolved?

What issues do need resolving?
....

Anger is a very real emotion, and is positive if used correctly. Jesus expressed anger in Mark 3:5 when he healed a withered hand on the Sabbath.

And when He had looked around at them with anger, being grieved by the hardness of their hearts, He said to the man, **"Stretch out your hand."** And he stretched it out, and his hand was restored as whole as the other.

Anger was a common response from Him when dealing with sin. Christ did not hide His feelings. Our challenge is learning to feel and express balanced, appropriate anger.

To throw things at another, stand over, or strike another is never appropriate, even when an apology is given afterwards. Any behavior that creates fear or intimidation needs to be evaluated and changed.

Consider the concepts expressed in the following scriptures.

Ephesians 4:32
32And be kind to one another, tenderhearted, forgiving one another, even as God in Christ forgave you.

Ephesians 4:26
26Be angry, and do not sin: do not let the sun go down on your wrath,

Ephesians 4:29,
29Let no corrupt word proceed out of your mouth, but what is good for necessary edification, that it may impart grace to the hearers.

Galatians 5:16-23
16I say then: Walk in the Spirit, and you shall not fulfill the lust of the flesh. 17For the flesh lusts against the Spirit, and the Spirit against the flesh; and these are contrary to one another, so that you do not do the things that you wish. 18But if you are led by the Spirit, you are not under the law.

19Now the works of the flesh are evident, which are: adultery, fornication, uncleanness, lewdness, 20idolatry, sorcery, hatred, contentions, jealousies, outbursts of wrath, selfish ambitions, dissensions, heresies, 21envy, murders, drunkenness, revelries, and the like; of which I tell you beforehand, just as I also told you in time past, that those who practice such things will not inherit the kingdom of God.

[22] But the fruit of the Spirit is love, joy, peace, longsuffering, kindness, goodness, faithfulness, [23] gentleness, self-control. Against such there is no law.

Romans 12:19-21
[19] Beloved, do not avenge yourselves, but rather give place to wrath; for it is written, "Vengeance is Mine, I will repay," says the Lord. [20] Therefore "If your enemy is hungry, feed him; If he is thirsty, give him a drink; For in so doing you will heap coals of fire on his head." [21] Do not be overcome by evil, but overcome evil with good.

Proverbs 14:29
[29] He who is slow to wrath has great understanding, But he who is impulsive exalts folly.

Proverbs 15:1
[1] A soft answer turns away wrath, But a harsh word stirs up anger.

Proverbs 19:11.
[11] The discretion of a man makes him slow to anger, And his glory is to overlook a transgression.

:: *Focus Point* ::

What are your thoughts on anger?

Do you consider it an issue for yourself or your partner?

Would your partner agree with your conclusions?

There are many means that people employ to gain control in conflict, an example being money. Perhaps other methods come to mind, even ways in which you have felt manipulated in your own relationships.

It is important to discuss these areas, perhaps even with a respected third party, as these issues do not just disappear when you get married. They are patterns that will interfere with your marriage, and usually worsen, if not dealt with.

In your marriage or other relationships, remember that conflict is normal and can help you grow. Often the conflict is not over the issue that started this disagreement, but other issues that have been buried.

We can deal with conflict in different ways. James Fairfied suggests five ways of dealing with it:

1. Winning is where you must win despite the cost.

2. Withdrawing is where you do not even try; you feel it is hopeless.

3. Yielding is where you allow the other his choice in an effort to   avoid the conflict.

4. Compromising is where you will find that you need to relent   a little in order to help the other to give a little. Neither you   nor the other wish to win all the time.

Or

5. Resolving conflicts is where the situation or attitude is changed   by direct and open discussion.

Conflict and Disagreement

:: ***Focus Point*** ::

What is your preferred way of dealing with conflict? Or perhaps the better question, how do you and your partner presently deal with conflict?

All of the five methods listed above have a place in marriage. While yielding and withdrawing do not produce results immediately, they still can be useful tools in conflict. When the situation is "heated," and one person withdraws temporarily, it can be beneficial as long as the situation is discussed later and resolved.

Although winning can feel good, it can sacrifice the relationship. You need to remember that personal relationships are as important, if not more so, than the goal you have in mind during the conflict.

In yielding, the goal is sacrificed in favor of the relationship. In compromising, you sacrifice some of your own desires. Resolving is the most desired style as it strengthens relationships. Below are some points to help resolve conflicts.

Instead of demanding to be heard, listen to the other person. When we want the other to change, we need to hear and understand them. This goes for both partners. Proverbs 18:13 says, ***"He who answers a matter before he hears it, It is folly and shame to him."***

Select an appropriate time for both partners to discuss the matter. Proverbs 15:23 says, ***"A man has joy by the answer of his mouth, And a word spoken in due season, how good it is!"***

Allow both people to describe the problem.

Discuss the areas of agreement and disagreement.

Most conflicts involve contributions from both sides. Admit and identify your contribution to the conflict and take responsibility for it. When a willingness to do this is seen, it is much easier to cooperate and discuss solutions. Make sure that you are not always the one waiting for the other to admit fault first.

Talk positively of appropriate behavioral changes. Allow each other to have opinions while being sensitive to the other's feelings. Be open to your partner's feelings and beware of defensiveness.

. . . .

Conflict and Disagreement

CHAPTER EIGHT
Sex and Intimacy

In today's world, the act of sex is widely misused and therefore has lost its real meaning. On vacation recently, I noticed that some public markets were filled with t-shirts portraying little red devils in all sorts of sexual positions. This sight is definitely not unusual in many cultures.

The media and Hollywood often present sex as crude and dirty. In some ways this causes us to believe that sex in marriage should only be boring. How can sex be fun if you are limited to one partner? We start to believe that God does not allow liberty in this area of our lives, and that liberty is synonymous with perversion.

Certainly God has placed parameters in this area, but these parameters allow us to feel a lot of freedom in the sexuality in our marriages. The most important thing for us to take hold of is that God created sex. And not just for procreation, but for enjoyment!

Today many share the view that it is better to try out sex with our loved one before marriage. That in doing so somehow we will know if the relationship will work. Since the sexual side of a relationship is something that develops with time and practice, this assumption holds little worth. Great sex is something that is attained over years of trust and commitment rather than swapped in initial encounters.

Sex, according to God's plan, was intended to provide a way of being close to one another and giving ourselves to the other. It is a way of communication whereby each person gets to know the other in a very intimate way.

We have varying ideas and knowledge regarding the sexual side of relationships.

The following scriptures reflect God's intention.

Song of Solomon 4:10-12
   ¹⁰*How delightful is your love, my sister, my bride!*
   How much more pleasing is your love than wine,
   and the fragrance of your perfume than any spice!
   ¹¹*Your lips drop sweetness as the honeycomb, my bride;*
   milk and honey are under your tongue.
   The fragrance of your garments is like that of Lebanon.
   ¹²*You are a garden locked up, my sister, my bride;*
   you are a spring enclosed, a sealed fountain.

Proverbs 5:18,19
   ¹⁸*Let your fountain be blessed,*
   and may you rejoice in the wife of your youth.
   ¹⁹*A loving doe, a graceful deer -*
   may her breasts satisfy you always,
   may you ever be captivated by her love.

Genesis 2:24,25.
   ²⁴*For this reason a man will leave his father and mother and be united to his wife, and they will become one flesh.*
   ²⁵*The man and his wife were both naked, and they felt no shame.*

These passages give us a glimpse of another part of God's nature. These verses in the Bible and others show that obviously God did not design sex as clinical and only for reproduction, but also to be fun and freeing.

Good sex is not automatic but is more of an achievement. Rather than basing our expectations on some recent movie, we need to accept the act as it is, as something to be worked at. This is far more beneficial.

Having seen the fiery, lusty sex scenes in movies, we can carry unrealistic expectations into our relationship and marriage. When people move from one relationship to another and do not refrain from sex before marriage, they can experience disappointment after disappointment.

One very honest young woman shared with me her thoughts, which are very common, "Who wants to be a Mr. and Mrs. Brady sitting up in bed in their sensible sleeping attire when other shows portray wild and passionate sex scenes?"

Unfortunately, these scenes of all night sex where both people wake from slumber looking beautiful are an unreal expectation that sets us up for failure.

Many newly married couples have intercourse and experience fulfillment right away while others work through different experiences. Some people fear failure or experience extreme self-consciousness, some fear pain or cannot believe that such an act can be tied to love.

Television makes it seem so easy and automatic, but a great sex life can take years to build. This is not always the case, but the sexual side of a relationship does generally require patience, understanding, and an ability to laugh and communicate.

The Bible presents a very real view of sex in 1 Corinthians 7:3-4,

> *3 The husband should fulfill his marital duty to his wife, and likewise the wife to her husband. 4 The wife's body does not belong to her alone but also to her husband. In the same way, the husband's body does not belong to him alone but also to his wife.*

Again we see another area of our lives that is more about giving than getting. In a good marriage, each partner recognizes that the other has a claim upon them sexually, and that their role is to provide pleasure rather than only seek it for themselves.

It is rare these days to enter marriage with no sexual experience. However, if a person does, they need to be congratulated. It is as

God intended. On the other hand, no one needs to feel condemned if they do not make it to the altar in this state.

Either way, your fears and concerns regarding sex in marriage should be discussed with one another. People struggle with a range of emotions from excitement to deep fear.

"Practice makes perfect" can be applied to the sexual side of our marriage relationship since great sex does not just happen naturally. Do not necessarily expect too much from the first sexual encounters. As a couple learns to respond to one another and develop the relationship, with patience, practice, and time, the sexual side of marriage gets better.

Couples must consider each other's needs for physical affection. People vary on their desire to be touched or to touch, and it is important to understand this about each other.

Neither partner has the right to inflict discomfort or pain. For the sexual side of a marital relationship to be successful, it is important that a husband and wife communicate what they like and appreciate. Exploring and practicing these likes is far more beneficial than reading a book on the topic!

Remember that every Christian marriage should symbolize the love of Christ for His church and God's love for His people. Look at Ephesians 5:32 and 33,

> *32This is a profound mystery-but I am talking about Christ and the church. 33However, each one of you also must love his wife as he loves himself, and the wife must respect her husband.*

It is vital that this area of your marriage "stay alive and work." Do not ever believe that this area is not important. Marriage breakdown happens often from the sexual side of a marriage not being fulfilling. We are fooling ourselves if we are thinking that a sexless marriage is acceptable.

The scripture presented earlier in this chapter, 1 Corinthians 7:3-4, indicates that even the sexual side of our marriage is about

Sex and Intimacy

giving and not getting. It should be our mutual intention to give our partner, rather than ourselves, pleasure. In doing so, both partners will enjoy this part of marriage.

In closing, let me remind you to discuss contraception. You need to be aware of the benefits and deficiencies of the various methods. Talk to other married couples and your doctor.

....

:: *Focus Point* ::

I remember a great story told to me by a friend. She had been attempting to explain the sexual act to her third child. The child's reaction was, "You mean you did that with Dad three times!!"

Looking back in your life, from where did you first hear or learn about the basics of reproduction, and how did you feel? Were or are you able to discuss sex or topics of a sexual nature with your parents?

How do you feel about marital sex and how (honestly) do you feel about your own body?

How does your past effect your outlook on your marriage? Is this an area that you are able to discuss with your partner?

While some have reservations about sex and various sexual acts, others feel totally liberal. It is important to consider one another's feelings. What do each of you see as your sexual roles in marriage?

Do you know of any differences in the way that you and your partner feel in this area?

....

CHAPTER NINE

Expectations

Every engaged couple experiences a sense of excitement that comes from the undertaking of a new adventure called marriage. However, you need to keep in mind that even though this adventure is new to you, it has been around for a long time.

As you advance in your marriage, you will experience hopes and difficulties. How you deal with these will determine the strength, fortitude, and closeness you and your spouse can have in marriage. This will also lay a foundation that you will draw from and build upon, whether good or bad.

You have probably seen things in your partner that you like and dislike. You have shared hopes, and noticed areas that will present difficulties. Earlier in this book I discussed areas of similarities and differences. Let's have another look at the how differences affect our relationships.

Differences can be divided into two groups, those that can be changed, and those that cannot. We discussed some areas that cannot be changed, such as one's age or race. Personal habits, sleeping late or getting up early, are areas that can be altered however.

All people go into a marriage with certain expectations. This is part of being human. Both you and your partner have expectations. For example, sleeping late on Saturday mornings, or showering first thing in the morning.

Twenty years into our marriage, Dean and I still have differences. I like the garage door to be closed while he wants it conveniently opened. To him, dirty clothes are to be strewn around the bedroom, while I like them in the hamper. The compromise is that they are stacked neatly in the bathroom next to the tub so that I can take them to the washer.

One of the recent changes we made is that if I am out of town the freshly washed clothes are piled in the hallway outside the laundry for all three boys - Dean and the two children. They are therefore handy to be taken as needed. It does not concern any of the Sweetman men that one has to leap over the clothing to get into the laundry, or that they are un-ironed!

As you discover your differences in expectations, you will also likely see traits of your personality. What expectations do your partner currently have that are different from your way of living? These often reveal each person's preconceived ideas about "marriage."

Often, people choose partners who they think can help them feel complete in themselves. Some do this purposefully while others are completely unaware of it. Some try to get too much "completion" out of their partner, which is detrimental to the marriage relationship.

Many times when we are feeling inadequate or depressed, we try to lean too heavily upon our partner. This is also true in times of crisis. Too much leaning on the other person tends to drive one's spouse away rather than closer.

Sometimes our spouse's differences can be threatening to us. This is especially true when you feel that in order for progress to occur, you have to be the one who adjusts your thinking.

In general, people approach life with a certain type of person in mind for their spouse. Usually the person you marry turns out to be anything but that idea you dreamt about all those years. So how do all your dreams and ideas come true? How do you achieve that oneness in marriage that is talked of so often?

We need to appreciate our spouse's differences and keep an attitude of acceptance and happiness. Matthew 7:3-5 says,

> *3 Why do you look at the speck in your brother's eye but do not notice the log that is in your own eye... 5 Take the log out of your own eye and then you will see clearly to take the speck out of your brother's eye.*

It is imperative for us to realize that the only relationship that can fulfill us is a relationship with Jesus Christ. Others can be a support, but only Christ fulfills. Even in realizing this, the tendency is to turn to our spouse rather than Christ to solve our problems. In Genesis 3:16 God shows this to us. To the woman He said,

16 "I will greatly multiply your sorrow and your conception; In pain you shall bring forth children; Your desire shall be for your husband, And he shall rule over you."

God tells us that our inclination as women will be to lean on our husbands. This is not His desire, but a consequence of the fall of mankind. When one develops a relationship with Christ, turning to Him needs to become the preference.

Remember, it is not our job to try to remodel our partner, but rather to discover and value the differences in him or her.

Below is a list of some common life crises or situations that can happen during a marriage. Take time to give these situations, and the changes that would occur in your marriage as a result, some thought. Perhaps you have already dealt with some of these in your life. Perhaps now you would deal with them differently.

. . . .

Your wife does not want to work in financial hardship.

You cannot afford a home for 5 years while friends seem to be zooming ahead in this area.

You have been informed that medically you cannot have children.

One partner wants more children than the other.
Wife wants to work while children are young.

Job loss (husband or wife) for extended period of time.

Wife earns more than husband.

You find yourself attracted to your partner's friend or another person in church.

Your in-laws are more involved in your lives and the decision- making processes than you desire, and they seem hostile towards you. However, your spouse does not see this.

Husband works Saturdays and nights while the children are still in elementary school, so many responsibilities fall on you.

Spouse loses interest in church.

....

    Believe it or not, these are all very typical and usually will affect us at some time or another in our marriage. We can easily avoid some of these when we look after our marriage and follow God's principles. Other scenarios are a part of our lives and we seem to have no choice. It is during these times that we really need to support and love one another and come into God's presence as often as we can. If we go after God, stay connected to our local church, and continue to work on our marriage, the crisis either passes or seems to become easier to handle.

    Understand that the husband is the covering for a marriage and family, but beyond this, God provides the local church as a covering. I have seen so many crises pass as couples and families have maintained their connection with their church even when they have not understood their pastor's advice.

    This is actually when submission is important. Submission

is not about times of agreement, but times of disagreement. We therefore don't necessarily agree or understand a decision or advice, but we recognize that under covering, whether husband or church, there is safety and God's plan for our lives.

Romans 12:9 says,

> *⁹Let love be without hypocrisy. Abhor what is evil. Cling to what is good.*

My New American Standard version titles this passage "Behave Like a Christian." It is what we are supposed to do. When we hurt we do not want to do the right thing, but following our feelings does not always build our marriages (or any relationship), particularly when we are offended.

We see dreams fulfilled and experience "oneness" in marriage when we come into a mutual understanding and accept our partner's differences rather than trying to make them into our "ideal." When we can become comfortable in ourselves and in the uniqueness of our partner, we begin to appreciate and value each other's strengths and weaknesses. This allows for an attitude of happiness to breed, and the marriage can flourish.

CHAPTER TEN
Goals and Visions

In my decision to marry, the only thing I had on my mind was the wedding ceremony and walking down the aisle. Who would be my bridesmaids? What would we all wear? Does Dean really love me?

It never occurred to me to consider such matters as culinary or domestic skills. I did not even think about these "limitations" prior to my marriage.

Fortunately for me, Dean had a huge sense of humor. One of his pair of dress pants came out of the washing machine looking like a pair of shorts. I insisted that he'd gained weight even though the label said "Dry Clean Only."

A benefit for me during this time was the great teaching from my church concerning vision and goal setting. The truth of how I could better myself by simply learning how to set goals. Obviously my marriage would benefit from this also, as vision gives us direction and purpose.

I have since learned that very few people set goals or have a vision for their marriage, as I didn't at the beginning of my marriage. In Proverbs 29:18, God speaks of all the lost people who have no vision experience.

> *[18] Where there is no revelation, the people cast off restraint; But happy is he who keeps the law.*

Without goals and vision, it is difficult, if not impossible, to find true fulfillment.

Goal setting doesn't have to be complicated. Goals can be

short-range or long-range. They can be for you individually, or for you as a couple. Sometimes the goals may be a joint venture that both your partner and you share. An example of an individual goal of mine at one stage that also enhanced my marriage was my learning how to cook.

I don't want to become too theoretical about this area, but to discuss one another's dreams, aspirations, and goals helps us make plans for our lives and see what endeavors to pursue.

Many people do have dreams and visions, but are wary of expressing them for fear of ridicule or criticism. However, when we come into the loving arena of marriage, become bold and share those desires that are closest to our hearts with our closest companion, our partner, in doing this, we build one another in faith and therefore can spur one another on.

Goals are like small steps that take you towards your vision. The small step can be to save a little money each week, for example $50. The weekly $50 may be going toward the deposit for your vision - a home of your own.

Of course goals can change as we mature or our circumstances shift, and yet the great thing about goals is that they offer direction and a sense of purpose. They help develop a marriage.

It is not that we need to sit down and write lists of our goals for life, but it is a good idea to regularly communicate these with each other to make certain that both partners are focusing in a similar direction. You may have the small steps organized, such as saving money, but while one is envisioning the house, the other may be seeing a new car!

Dean and I often find that tension increases in our marriage when we are unaware of each other's goals or ambitions. When we share these, we can help each other move toward achievement. Alternatively, we may find that the desired goal is not good for our family at this time, and so it is abandoned for the immediate future, perhaps forever. No matter what it is, discussing our goals bring clarity into our relationship.

It may be redecorating a room in the house, or changing the

Goals and Visions

direction of a career, but as I have shared my ideas with my partner, I have found that not only has he been supportive, but also his input has brought greater success.

An excellent way to develop goals is to have a vision for your marriage. This statement needs to be specific as well as positive. Keep it free from too many details. Keep it simple.

Since goals move you toward a vision, let's discuss vision a bit more. Vision can be described in several ways, but I want to discuss it with a view of seeing the invisible while being in the process of making it visible. In this way, you see a picture in your mind of the way you'd like things to be in the future. This "picture" doesn't yet exist, you are "seeing" what isn't real as if it were real. A Godly vision has God's direction, and it recognizes God's power.

Because vision is specific, it gives shape to and helps develop the marriage. To have a vision for your marriage is to have a realistic dream for what you, your partner, and your marriage can become under God's direction. Moreover, by focusing on where you're headed, it will help keep you from getting enmeshed in the past or even the present. Jeremiah 29:11 is a promise of God to give you a hope and a future.

> **11 For I know the thoughts that I think toward you, says the LORD, thoughts of peace and not of evil, to give you a future and a hope.**

Envision your future with this promise in mind.

Below are some examples of marriage goals. These are basic goals, but nevertheless address issues that cause strife in marriages:

> I will listen to my partner's viewpoint, discuss it, and complete a task the way my partner would at least once before encouraging them to do it my way.

> I will work towards admitting when I am wrong and be less

defensive.

I will hear the other person totally before interjecting my point of view.

I will be more flexible and spontaneous regarding visiting and having company. I will do this with a great attitude.

I will show my love more in actions, both verbally and non-verbally. I will compliment my partner at least once a day and ask them how I can help.

....

:: *Focus Point* ::

You and your partner each think of a great vision statement for your marriage, then compare them. Perhaps you cannot think of one, but at least you are both discussing and sharing ideas for your future. One of the main keys is that it should revolve around you being together.

What goals do you have for your marriage and how do these compare with those of your partner? Have you ever discussed what each of you expect from your marriage?

Remember, a goal needs to be achievable, reasonable and consider a time limit.

Select one of your goals and establish a plan to reach it. Remember that it can be re-evaluated and so be bold.

Would these goals also be a priority to your partner?

Other things to consider with goal-setting are:

Do you feel that any of these goals you've listed were given to you by God, or are they just a great idea?

What will it cost you financially to fulfill these goals?

Are these truly your goals, or are they traditions passed down by your family?

Are these goals really significant to both of you?
. . . .

CHAPTER ELEVEN

Responsibility

As a couple it becomes very important to decide who is going to do what in regard to responsibilities. Each couple needs to decide who is going to complete tasks without necessarily being influenced by tradition, family, or social setting.

It is very easy to assume that the wife needs to fulfill all household responsibilities because that was the way it was in your upbringing. These assumptions typically can cause friction in a marriage.

Roles of men and women have changed dramatically over the years. Some people think that women need to stay home and be a homemaker, wife, and mother. That this is her role. The other extreme is to have her in the workforce while her husband tends to the home and the children. There is much variety in between these, including equal rights and responsibilities.

Roles can change in a marriage as children arrive, careers change, and priorities shift. We may try designating certain responsibilities only to find that it is not working and therefore we need to be open again to more changes for the sake of the marriage and family. Children's security comes from feeling the security of mom and dad's relationship. A big key in sorting out responsibility is always considering each other.

Each of us needs to consider the roles that we see each other playing in marriage. Do you see yourself always in the workforce or do you endeavor a career change down the road? Have you considered that your partner may be planning a different path for the future?

What thoughts about roles and responsibilities will you/did you bring into your marriage? Consider the influence of your own family and background. Are your ideas different from that of your

SALT & PEPPER: you go together

partner?

Here are some statements and questions that tend to cause confusion in marriage.

. . . .

These statements should be discussed with your partner.

The responsibility of the husband is his work, while the responsibility of the wife is the home and children.

The husband is the head of the family. Ephesians 5:23 says, **"For the husband is head of the wife, as also Christ is head of the church; and He is the Savior of the body."**

The wife should not be employed.

The husband should help with housework.

Finances and money matters should be planned together.

The wife should have her own money to spend whether she has earned it or her husband has given it to her.

The husband has to do the yard work.

The wife is always the one to cook or bake.

How much money can one spend without consulting the other?

Either partner can initiate sexual activity.

The wife is just as responsible as the husband for disciplining the children.

It is the responsibility of the mother to teach values to the children.

A husband or wife should not socialize separately once married.

. . . .

In Ephesians 5:21-33, marriage is compared to Christ and his relationship to the church. Therefore according to this passage it is essential that we consider each other.

^{21}submitting to one another in the fear of God. ^{22}Wives, submit to your own husbands, as to the Lord. ^{23}For the husband is head of the wife, as also Christ is head of the church; and He is the Savior of the body. ^{24}Therefore, just as the church is subject to Christ, so let the wives be to their own husbands in everything. ^{25}Husbands, love your wives, just as Christ also loved the church and gave Himself for her, ^{26}that He might sanctify and cleanse her with the washing of water by the word, ^{27}hat He might present her to Himself a glorious church, not having spot or wrinkle or any such thing, but that she should be holy and without blemish. ^{28}So husbands ought to love their own wives as their own bodies; he who loves his wife loves himself. ^{29}For no one ever hated his own flesh, but nourishes and cherishes it, just as the Lord does the church. ^{30}For we are members of His body, of His flesh and of His bones. ^{31}"For this reason a man shall leave his father and mother and be joined to his wife, and the two shall become one flesh." ^{32}This is a great mystery, but I speak concerning Christ and the church. ^{33}Nevertheless let each one of you in particular so love his own wife as himself, and let the wife see that she respects her husband.

Despite it sounding old fashioned, from a scriptural viewpoint, a woman's obedience to her husband is inseparably related to her obedience to the Lord. Really, to obey one is to obey the other. Revelation of this truth leads to a wife finding fulfillment in her marriage. But it is also vital that the husband love his wife as Christ loved the church. He gave his life up for the sake of ours.

It is the role of the husband as "head of the wife" to not just protect her, but release the potential within her. This is the meaning of "headship" as seen in the above passage - releaser of life and talents. One translation expresses his role as that of a fountainhead. This therefore presents many options for a wife beyond keeping a home and raising children. It is through his headship that she can grow and explore options.

Submission is often wrongly thought of as for the wife only. Yes, it is good that she allows her husband the final say in a decision, but to not have an opinion or to never have a say makes her unnecessary.

As said previously, submission does concern those times of conflict or disagreement when one has to give way to the other. Marriages flourish when partners consider one another rather than each trying to always have their way.

However, in a good marriage, decisions are made according to each partner's wellbeing, wisdom, and knowledge. The husband will be making decisions with this in mind. There are many decisions that Dean now trusts me to make and then there are others that I do not wish to make alone. We have grown to trust each other in certain areas, and so feel comfortable with the other to decide certain issues.

If he is out of town, he trusts me to make certain decisions for the household without having to consult him. The basement flooded and so I called friends who knew the calls to make. Dean, being out of town, was not in a place to make any decisions for this crisis except to console me amid laughter later on. He came home to huge fans blowing air and tripped fuses throughout the house.

During Dean's travels, I will wait on some decisions to be able to talk with him. Perhaps it can wait, or it involves a large sum of money. Perhaps it affects our future, or members of our church.

To be confident with decisions is great, but to constantly act alone without consultation can only create friction. We are acting more as a single person with no regard for the other, and are not building closeness in our relationship.

Some decisions are best made by the man, while others are best made by the woman. Rarely does a man want to decide the shopping list, but he usually does want to add some items.

Often an issue is important to one but not to the other. As long as there is a mutual understanding and consideration of the other, submission is taking place.

A wife needs to always honor, love, and respect her man, allowing him his God-given authority. She chooses to submit to her husband and a man cannot make his wife comply. Submission is a choice. It is something that women choose to do.

In Bible times, culturally, women were often viewed as unworthy of education and necessary only for reproduction and tasks. This is not God's view or plan for us. The Ephesians 5 passage is revolutionary for its time because of its acknowledgement of and care for women. A clear picture of submission is presented to us through the relationship of Jesus Christ the Son, and His father. It was a twofold relationship with Christ being subject to God. John 5:19 says,

> *19Then Jesus answered and said to them, "Most assuredly, I say to you, the Son can do nothing of Himself, but what He sees the Father do; for whatever He does, the Son also does in like manner."*

Yet he was equal to God. John 10:30 says,

> *30"I and My Father are one."*

Submissiveness carries no hint of inferiority. 1 Peter 3:7 says,

> *⁷Husbands, likewise, dwell with them with understanding, giving honor to the wife, as to the weaker vessel, and as being heirs together of the grace of life, that your prayers may not be hindered.*

Inferiority is as irrelevant to the wife as it is to Christ.

Often due to mistreatment of a scripture we want to then eradicate its application from our lifestyles. The word submission has become a word that causes many to roll their eyes or shudder. It carries a wrong meaning of confinement and having no rights. However, if a husband is fulfilling his role we will flourish.

Even if a husband is not doing all that he should, God's word teaches the following in 1 Peter 3:1-2,

> *¹Wives, likewise, be submissive to your own husbands, that even if some do not obey the word, they, without a word, may be won by the conduct of their wives, ²when they observe your chaste conduct accompanied by fear.*

I have often noticed that a wife can become critical of her husband if he does not wish to be as involved in church as she does, or if he does not display his spirituality as she sees fit. Perhaps he is more of a phlegmatic nature in comparison to her more choleric nature. Often a man can be repelled from increased involvement in church due to his wife's attitude and judgment of him.

Some husbands just give up trying to lead their wives anywhere because no matter the decision, she will not comply. She feels that she always knows best. Submission cannot be forced but it is a choice. It is an inner attitude and a step of faith. Hebrews 11:6 says,

Without faith it is impossible to please God.

Wives need to allow a husband to lead. Wives need to step aside at times and display confidence in their husbands. Wives

Responsibility

also need to know that a quick decision is not necessarily a good decision. Submission is not necessarily about being right or wrong, but is God's provided covering. Spirituality also is not necessarily being in church every service or speaking Christian jargon, but rather living as Scripture advises. As we mature as believers we should be more relatable to people. There is much freedom in Biblical submission as seen in Proverbs 31:10-31.

[10] Who can find a virtuous wife? For her worth is far above rubies. [11] The heart of her husband safely trusts her So he will have no lack of gain. [12] She does him good and not evil All the days of her life. [13] She seeks wool and flax, And willingly works with her hands. [14] She is like the merchant ships, She brings her food from afar. [15] She also rises while it is yet night, And provides food for her household, And a portion for her maidservants. [16] She considers a field and buys it; From her profits she plants a vineyard. [17] She girds herself with strength, And strengthens her arms. [18] She perceives that her merchandise is good, And her lamp does not go out by night. [19] She stretches out her hands to the distaff, And her hand holds the spindle. [20] She extends her hand to the poor, Yes, she reaches out her hands to the needy. [21] She is not afraid of snow for her household, For all her household is clothed with scarlet. [22] She makes tapestry for herself; Her clothing is fine linen and purple. [23] Her husband is known in the gates, When he sits among the elders of the land. [24] She makes linen garments and sells them, And supplies sashes for the merchants. [25] Strength and honor are her clothing; She shall rejoice in time to come. [26] She opens her mouth with wisdom, And on her tongue is the law of kindness. [27] She watches over the ways of her household, And does not eat the bread of idleness. [28] Her children rise up and call her blessed; Her

husband also, and he praises her: ²⁹*"Many daughters have done well, But you excel them all."* ³⁰*Charm is deceitful and beauty is passing, But a woman who fears the LORD, she shall be praised.* ³¹*Give her of the fruit of her hands, And let her own works praise her in the gates.*

This passage illustrates many doors through which women can walk due to her submissiveness and an honoring and loving husband, whether it is with family, career, or ministry.

Through submission, an environment is created through which a woman can express her individuality. It is God's way of drawing upon her gifts while not burdening her with the responsibility of leadership and provision.

Over the years I have developed a confidence in myself and my abilities that has surprised me. This is because a wife predominantly draws her esteem from the way a husband treats her. A husband predominantly draws his esteem from his work or career.

Husbands are commanded to love their wives. This is measured not so much by what a man does or feels, but rather by the sacrifice of one's self. Everything Christ did was for His bride. Galatians 2:20 says,

²⁰*I have been crucified with Christ; it is no longer I who live, but Christ lives in me; and the life which I now live in the flesh I live by faith in the Son of God, who loved me and gave Himself for me.*

This is a high expectation, but it is attainable as we realize we are to live by faith and Christ lives within us. Mistakes will be made, but to step out and do nothing means that nothing is learned and no progress made. Therefore, the husband that leads makes decisions that are faith-based.

The authority that he exercises is not really that of his own, but given by God. Therefore it needs to be used wisely.

The role of head and an expectation for submission cannot happen because of demand but is won. Jesus displayed many qualities in His lifetime, from protector to clear leadership. The husband's responsibility to his wife is to treat her as Christ treats the church, knowing that he is caring for his wife's sanctification and walk with the Lord.

What are some of the ways in which a husband can demonstrate his love? With much affirmation that she is needed, that she is unique and appreciated. That she is a priority and is given attention and time. That she is given security through stable income. He helps her physically with the children and housework and does not dismiss her as overly emotional, but recognizes her needs and feelings.

Christ is head of His church and speaks of the members giving to and into one another. Christ sees this also for our marriages. As we acknowledge this concept and submit, Christ releases us through our local church. As we submit to one another in our marriages and allow our husband's headship, we experience a similar flourishing.

:: *Focus Point* ::

Marriage is about giving to and receiving from one another.

Have you realized the talents or areas of expertise that your partner brings into your marriage?

Who makes the majority of decisions in your relationship and are you comfortable with this?

When making decisions, several things should be considered:
- Who is more qualified to make that decision?
- Does one partner know more in a given situation?
- Is one more expert than the other in the area concerned?
- What is the reason for one having more say than the other?

- What time and opportunities are involved?

Decision-making needs to be done carefully and considerately as it can lead to feelings of resentment.

What do you consider to be a major decision? Would your partner agree?

Look at the list below and check the situations in which you want input. If you want your partner's input, check twice.

Choice of church
Choice of friends
Choice of work/career
Choice of home
Choice of vacations
Child rearing techniques
Choice of car
Choice in expenditure
Home decorating
Choice of dress
Number of children
TV/entertainment

What will you do when you disagree, and yet, a decision has to be made?

When do you feel that you have "the right" to overlook your partner's decision?

Will you make decisions if your partner will not?

Have you considered that perhaps they are just slower to arrive at a conclusion, or are just hesitant?

Responsibility

CHAPTER TWELVE

Money

Finances and the pressure that it puts on a marriage are one of the greatest reasons for marriage breakdown today. We each bring a financial mindset plus financial commitments into the marriage. Our financial mindsets can be very different from one another. For example, you may never have experienced financial hardship but your partner may have battled this since childhood. Perhaps you are one that constantly fears you are not going to have enough finances to pay the bills.

Because money is an essential part of living, it is important that financial adjustments are made by both partners in a marriage. It is also good to realize that God's plan for abundance includes the financial realm. Many people fear money and many believe it to be evil, but this is not so. The mistake with money is placing reliance upon it to bring us happiness and security rather than God.

When you marry, there will be new financial responsibilities that are all your own. No authority such as parents should direct or monitor you; it is your responsibility as a married couple. Together you will need to plan ahead, budget, and anticipate future needs so that you are in control of your money and not vice versa. For many newly married couples this can take a bit of work.

For proper financial management, it is necessary to know what each other is thinking and planning in regard to spending money. All money brought into your home should be regarded as collective, and both partners should know of the money's destination. Goals and priorities regarding money need to be set, and money is only spent after its destination has been mutually agreed upon. Of course it is understood that goals need to always be flexible in view of the fact that circumstances change.

There are two categories for spending money - necessities and wants. Necessities are obviously the priority and include such things as tithe, rent or mortgage, food, recurring bills (telephone, etc.), transportation, basic clothing, and pocket money.

Wants are TVs, stereos, a house, expensive clothing, microwaves, or even the bar of chocolate at the supermarket. There are many things that we want to be necessities, but in the early years of marriage, we need to understand that this is all they are - wants not needs.

So many of us launch out and buy an article such as a big screen TV or a too-expensive car on credit, only to find that years down the track that we do not even remember what we're still paying for.

A two-income family is advised, if possible, to use the husband's income for needs and the wife's income for wants. If you operate with a single-family income, needs are always a priority over wants.

Money in and of itself is not bad. It is not being able to control your spending habits, or when money starts to control you, that often causes people to label it as evil.

In marriage, we need to be careful that we do not use money as a source of control or as a source of status. It must never control you. You should not be continually distrusting your partner with money, going over the receipts all the time, or questioning them. It is also important not to overspend as a means of keeping up with friends and neighbors.

::: Focus Point :::

Consider your financial priorities. Think of the five areas where you are currently spending your money in order of importance.

Should you make any changes to your current priorities?

Your partner and you need to write out a list of financial priorities for your marriage. Take into consideration leisure and recreation.

Money

A decision needs to be made as to who is going to oversee your finances. In our society today, the traditional role of the man being the chief money earner is no longer necessarily true. Both man and wife need to be involved in the budgeting, planning, and spending.

Who will pay the bills and handle the checks? Perhaps it is a task that you will do together.

Since it is a good idea to be aware of the cost of items, I have included a section below for the men to complete entitled "For Women" while the women need to complete the section that is titled "For Men." Fill in what you think the item costs.

FOR MEN (women complete)
Men's occupational outfit _____
Haircut _____
Week's groceries for two _____
Lawn mower _____
A midsize car _____
Cost of hobby, ex: golf clubs, gym membership _____
Complete car service _____
New seat covers for a car _____
Two tickets for a sporting event _____
A dining room suite _____
Weekly spending for lunches, movies, etc. _____

FOR WOMEN (men complete)
Woman's bathing suit _____
Color with cut _____
Week's groceries for two _____
Pair of living room drapes _____
A midsize car _____
Cost of hobby, ex: tennis, gym membership _____
Complete car service _____

Manicure plus pedicure _____
Monthly beauty supplies _____
A dining room suite _____
Weekly spending for lunches, movies, etc. _____

. . . .

Financial Backgrounds

How did you feel about money as you were growing up? Did you feel secure that there was enough in your household, were you conscious of being financially better or worse off than your friends, were you the rich kid in your class? Perhaps was there too much emphasis placed on money in your family?

Dean and I both grew up experiencing financial hardship at times. However, our reactions to these circumstances were very different. While he was determined to enjoy life and spend, I constantly feared not having enough money.

Often the person that we marry has a very different financial background from us. Can you see this as causing some conflict in your marriage?

There are some great scriptures with principles that you can utilize regarding finances. Some of them are as follows:

Proverbs 11:24-25
24 There is one who scatters, yet increases more; And there is one who withholds more than is right, But it leads to poverty. 25 The generous soul will be made rich, And he who waters will also be watered himself.

Proverbs 13:11
11 Wealth gained by dishonesty will be diminished, But he who gathers by labor will increase.

Proverbs 13:22
22 A good man leaves an inheritance to his children's children, But the wealth of the sinner is stored up for the

righteous.

Proverbs 22:1
> [1] A good name is to be chosen rather than great riches, Loving favor rather than silver and gold.

Proverbs 22:4
> [4] By humility and the fear of the LORD Are riches and honor and life.

Proverbs 22:7
> [7] The rich rules over the poor, And the borrower is servant to the lender.

Proverbs 21:5
> [5] The plans of the diligent lead surely to plenty, But those of everyone who is hasty, surely to poverty.

Hebrews 13:5-6
> [5] Let your conduct be without covetousness; be content with such things as you have. For He Himself has said, "I will never leave you nor forsake you." [6] So we may boldly say: "The LORD is my helper; I will not fear. What can man do to me?"

Matthew 6:19-21
> [19] "Do not lay up for yourselves treasures on earth, where moth and rust destroy and where thieves break in and steal; [20] but lay up for yourselves treasures in heaven, where neither moth nor rust destroys and where thieves do not break in and steal. [21] For where your treasure is, there your heart will be also.

Budgeting Suggestions That May Work For You

Plan your budget and make decisions together. Figures and plans should be known by both of you.

Define your financial goals, and know why you are trying to budget.

Know what you need to spend regularly before you plan a budget.

Be practical and look at the whole family's spending habits.

Are you wise with credit cards? Many people are better to take all credit cards out of their wallets except one for emergencies. It could be wise to cancel them!

Keep within a set allowance for yourself each week. Learn to say no.
Plan for big expenses, such as taxes, insurance, and vacation. Put aside an amount each month to meet these expenses.
Know between the two of you who is in charge of what. For example, car expenses and housekeeping.

You should be allowed to spend your budget as you wish, though it is a good idea to take a complete inventory every so often to examine your spending habits. Do not demand detailed accounts of one another's spending.

Have a checking account that you deposit into each payday to cover expenses.

Do not cheat your budget. If you cannot afford it, do not spend it or charge it!

Do not carry around too much cash.
Evaluate your budget regularly. You need to be realistic and enjoy life.

Your budget may not work at the first try. Revise it and try again. Ask for help from someone who is respected in this area. Make sure you set aside money for things that go towards building your marriage, such as a weekend away or a night out as a couple.

CHAPTER THIRTEEN
Parents and In-Laws

When we marry, we not only gain a partner, but also a new family. We become an in-law. What does this mean? Do you realize that in-laws also include the siblings of our future spouse as well? It is just not the mother and father of our future partner.

We can carry an ideal image of the perfect in-law relationship - sweet little granny and grandpa with snowy white hair that will drop in and clean the house, and regularly mind the grand babies whenever we feel the need of a night out! We suppose that they have nothing to do but look after our demands! We assume that they have no other life and forget that they are often still in the workforce or planning escapades that were not possible while raising us.

There is so much more to these relationships than them just being a free baby sitting service. Exodus 18:13-24 describes an incidence between Moses and his father-in-law, Jethro. Jethro gives constructive advice to Moses, who is humble and wise enough to act on it. Are we willing to hear the wisdom of, or at least willing to listen to, our parents or parents-in-law?

The Book of Ruth displays another example of an exceptional in-law relationship. On the death of her husband, father-in-law, and brother-in-law, Ruth leaves her family and familiar surroundings to accompany her sad and bitter mother-in-law to a foreign land. Obviously, she carried a deep love and respect for Naomi to complete such a courageous act, and God blesses her greatly.

We can look at Bible personalities and think that they were extra spiritual or supernaturally enabled to do great feats. Why else would a woman leave her family, home, and culture to follow an old woman to an unknown family and culture that worshipped a

SALT & PEPPER: you go together

different god?

Perhaps it was simply that they made wise choices. Some of the dilemmas they faced are not so different from those we face today.

Sometimes in a new relationship, and in our youthfulness and excitement, we fail to acknowledge the wealth of information that an older generation has acquired. With new technology and the continual influx of new ideas, why listen to an older generation?

The fact is that marriage has been around since the beginning of time. It originated in the Bible, and to listen to anyone that has made a marriage last beyond twenty or so years is a worthy time investment. Even more so to be around a couple that has stayed committed thirty, forty, fifty years plus.

We know a great couple in their eighties that have been committed to our church since its commencement. They started attending when we were just twenty members and have stayed committed until recently. They came along with us one growth move to another, building after building.

Their great age has caused them now to move away to be in close proximity to family, but in those early days, Betty knitted caps when our building was too small to house all the children mid-winter. She opened her home to our women and small groups. Mort would repeatedly bring in books of Biblical knowledge to help us prepare messages and stock our college library. They have shared their testimony in our Bible School and are one of the most loved couples in our church.

Until recently they walked through our church doors most Sundays, proud to be a part of an ever-growing young church, 1500 members strong. Mort was seen in our Starbucks café before each meeting, buying his coffee and chatting to the many young couples, being a friend to anyone, and not condescending to their youthfulness in any way.

They have been married for about sixty years and love nothing more than to be around the young life of our church. They watch with anticipation and excitement as our young people often find a marriage partner in the House of God. (As previously stated, it is so important that partners in a marriage enjoy the same or a similar style of worship. So what better place to find a marriage partner than in the House of God!)

However, more than anything, I have to mention that many of us, including Dean and myself, deeply respect this couple who has held to their commitment to marriage and love each other deeply. They have fantastic relationships with their grown children and grandchildren.

There are many for whom I hold a deep admiration, but this couple has been loyal to us since the very start of our church, even in Dean's and my youthfulness as new ministers in Atlanta. They themselves are parents, in-laws, and grandparents.

In our marriages, it is so easy to just assume that we are going to "whisk" our new partner away from their parents and family - that we will not really have to develop a relationship with these people called in-laws that are attached to our partner. However, this is not so.

This person with whom you fell in love is very much a part of the two parents and siblings, whom we often try to run from. Apart from biology, years have been spent together and thought processes, culture, ideas, and habits have become a part of this person to whom you committed your life.

The Bible talks of leaving family to cleave to your spouse in Ephesians 5:31,

31For this reason a man shall leave his father and mother and be joined to his wife, and the two shall become one flesh.

This does not conclude that you can now remove your new partner from any future ties with their family. It also does not mean that family is still a priority over the marriage. It is so important to discuss our ideas and thoughts regarding these matters rather than making assumptions.

It does mean that the newly married couple needs to commit

to one another and defer to one another before other family. Honor each other's opinions and needs before other family. This can be difficult, as many of the decisions required in a new marriage are things you may not have dealt with before. Therefore we can have a tendency to go to something familiar, mom and dad. Apart from perhaps seeking out advice, the new couple needs to venture out and create a new life where they start to make decisions together without interference from parents.

Regarding in-laws, we do need to remember that often we are dealing with an older generation and we need to understand that habits are harder to change as we age. As much as the young couple are starting off on an exciting new life parents are facing the closing of an era for themselves - their child is leaving.

What does this mean? On a positive note it means less cleaning, less cooking, no waiting up late at night for children to make it home. On the other hand though, there is the revelation that a child is moving on. Many parents view the completion of the raising of their children as the end of an era. They have to adjust and find new interests if they have not already done so.

I am a strong advocate for men and women developing interests outside of their children. To invest in our families is very important, but to forget that we are people apart from being parents is foolish. What does that mean? In Genesis, God created man and woman and not just moms and dads. We were created with much to offer beyond being a great mom and dad. Genesis 1:27-28 says,

> *^{27}So God created man in His own image; in the image of God He created him; male and female He created them. ^{28}Then God blessed them, and God said to them "Be fruitful and multiply; fill the earth and subdue it; have dominion over the fish of the sea, over the birds of the air, and over every living thing that moves on the earth."*

In this passage, we see that God created both man and woman

Parents and In-Laws

to work, take dominion, and reproduce.

Proverbs 31:28-31 presents a woman that has many interests beyond her family and yet her family highly esteems her.

> **^{28}Her children rise up and call her blessed; Her husband also, and he praises her: ^{29}"Many daughters have done well, But you excel them all." ^{30}Charm is deceitful and beauty is passing, But a woman who fears the LORD, she shall be praised. ^{31}Give her of the fruit of her hands, And let her own works praise her in the gates.**

And so even as a newly married wife, think ahead. As a new mom, plan ahead. What are your interests? Could you, or would you, pursue a career or a hobby? You may not be ready to pursue your ideas now, but the time may come when you will. Of course plans change and the input of your husband and family is vital, but it is always important to look ahead.

Nevertheless in a new marriage, it is important that both parties let go. The young couple needs to cleave and commit to one another, making decisions together, and holding to these without allowing family to interfere. The parents also must let their children go. The process of separation does not have to be abrupt, but rather can be gradual.

As a parent or in-law, realize that the new spouse naturally may be concerned for the parental family. The newly married couple needs to be mindful that family ties are normal and important, and that rejection of them will only bring pain to everyone.

Parents will not automatically stop being interested in their children, and their help can be a wonderful thing. Often parents want to help in various ways, like financially with home buying or setting up the home. Occasionally there is the offer of cheap accommodation, all within the one home with the parents. All of these offers need to be given careful consideration. They can be helpful, or they can cripple us in the maturation process of the new marriage, emotionally, financially, and in the closeness and establishment of the new marriage.

Financial shortcuts are not always the best option. At the start of a marriage the priority needs to be toward one another and not money. We are sowing into each other and adjusting to the new relationship, and we prolong the transition by having excess family in the midst. What we sometimes see as beneficial may not be so in the long term. Part of the confidence that we gain in our marriages is through what we accomplish on our own.

Another scenario is when money is lent to help establish a young couple, either for a home, furnishings, or a car. Often despite good intentions, the process of cleaving to one another in the new marriage becomes complicated and cloudy. This can set up a pattern of the parents coming to the rescue, and so when other needs arise, the young couple look for support rather than having built wisdom and confidence to solve dilemmas of their own. They cleave to the wrong source, their parents, rather than God and each other.

Some couples twenty years down the track are still attempting to separate from their families. The intention was not to be so. Emotions are too intertwined and priorities and opinions are clouded in situations like this.

Adam and Eve worked together in the garden creating a future for themselves and learning life's lessons. They leapt at an opportunity that they thought would make life easier, that of more knowledge. They disregarded God's wisdom and made a decision that they assumed would make them more knowledgeable and therefore make life easier. This is often not the case, and we need to think carefully before making decisions that simply make the future look financially or physically easier.

Your main focus is the development of your relationship with your spouse, and so shortcuts to homeownership, financial security, and cars need to be evaluated carefully. In fact, I strongly advise the input of your pastor or a marriage counselor in any case or situation.

Too many times engaged couples have come in for a pre-marriage session, excited that parents are lending deposits for a

Parents and In-Laws

home or some similar venture. They are not open to discuss this, as they are consumed by the desire for goods and wealth. They are busy informing rather than hearing. They become dull and closed to advice. Minds are already made up. A fast so-called solution that often looks like the hand of God has appeared. Sometimes it is, sometimes it isn't.

How fantastic is the acquirement of homes, cars, furnishings, and indeed money itself. They bring along happiness and excitement. 1 Timothy 6:10 says,

¹⁰For the love of money is a root of all kinds of evil, for which some have strayed from the faith in their greediness, and pierced themselves through with many sorrows.

As already stated in the chapter on money, money in itself is not evil, but the obsession over it is. In fact, we need money to survive in this world. Just as our relationship with God relies on faith, so our survival depends on food and other essentials which require money.

Many of the young married couples, and even singles, in our church have become home owners or bought nice cars, but it has not been because of loans from parents. Rather it has been the sound Biblical teaching on finances by our leadership. The team has taken them on a journey where they have discovered the possibility of making money work for them rather than vice versa. They have been taught concerning tithing, that it is something that everyone needs to do rather than thinking that they cannot afford to.

And so, often after church on Sunday, we hear the excited yells for help as another young person or couple is excitedly moving into their first home.

But the marriage relationship should always be the priority. Too much pressure with loans early days can be destructive.

Apart from finances, there are also decisions to make regarding times of celebration. Whom do we visit for Thanksgiving, and then

SALT & PEPPER: you go together

Christmas, and then birthdays? The list grows.

These priorities will need to adjust particularly as children arrive. Dragging the carload of kids from one relative to the next can make one dread these so-called special occasions! I would often sit down at the end of Christmas day surrounded by wrapping paper and gifts, and realized that I had actually forgotten that it was Christmas Day!

Complications also arise due to ever-extending step relationships, as some families face crisis, divorce, and remarriage.

To plan together as a couple is important. To compromise early days only creates tension down the track. However, be aware that some parents are on their own, and so we can be thoughtful and perhaps organize a time together on a day close to the occasion. Firmness is better and more effective than hostility. Gradual breakaways rather than sudden reactions need to be put in place. We want to build a future of harmony rather than strife.

For Dean and myself, in our early years Christmas Day became one long list of lunches - a couple of hours here and a couple of hours there. After several years, and the arrival of babies, we commenced celebrating this day before, during, and after the actual holiday. Our boys loved this as the gifts went forever.

To work with other siblings is also important, as each family has needs and priorities. The main idea is to keep communicating and hearing the others' thoughts.

Always, as we should do with any person, look to the good points with parents and in-laws. We need to understand that in times when they seem too concerned with our affairs that they are probably sincerely interested in our welfare. We hold the choice of accepting it graciously, ignoring it, or following it. Rarely is there reason to reject family.

....

:: *Focus Point* ::

Following are some very important questions concerning family and in-laws. You need to consider these questions and share your answers with your partner.

Read the following scripture. What does it mean to you? It is written in both Ephesians 5:31 and Matthew 19:5. ***"For this reason a man shall leave his father and mother and be joined to his wife, and the two shall become one flesh."***

Describe your parents' reaction to your plans for marriage. Do you expect it to change?

Examine your relationship with your parents honestly. Are there any emotional ties or expectancies that interfere with your relationship with your partner? What is their opinion on this?

If your parents wish to contribute to your start in marriage financially, what would be their expectations?

Describe your present relationship with your parents. Has it changed over your life? How do you think they see your partner?

What do you think your in-laws think of you?

Is there anything about your partner's parents that you really dislike or like?

What have you done recently to express your appreciation of both sets of parents? How recently did this occur?

....

CHAPTER FOURTEEN
When Crises Strike!

"Strike" is an understatement. Probably a better term is "When Crises Slugs You." To me, our crises could be likened to repeated blows by a softball bat. At least that is what it felt like. Day after day of pushing on despite the pain of loss and confusion.

We were not so different from other people. Crises come unexpectedly and with little warning. They seem unfair, and yet holding onto this thought does not help in any way at all.

Crises arrive in many forms, whether it is divorce, death, bankruptcy, ill health, the collapse of a career, a major move, or a rebellious family member or friend. Crises hit us all, despite status, culture, or age. No matter what it is, life will never seem fair.

Crises are often unexplainable. Our best option is to press into our Maker. Through this, we realize that He provides us with wellbeing and that there is no better way. Even in this, we need to understand that the victory may not be in the form of what we ordered, but there is a bigger picture that only our Lord can see. And so we need to hang on, looking to our Maker, knowing that He has a plan for us and He knows us better than we know ourselves.

I was someone who thought that I would never experience marriage breakdown. I came from a family that did not promote divorce. I was used to financial hardship, but it was something that I did not want in my marriage. And yet it all happened. Did I know that Dean was unhappy? Did I realize that I was miserable? I was only aware that we were two people trying to make life work. Many would have described us as a typical "good couple" who were faithful church members.

Our marriage deteriorated several years into its existence. In fact, it would be better to say that most of our world collapsed, my husband's health, our finances, and our ministry. I had no job, and even our home was two halves of a house that had been "dumped" and stuck back together in my tolerant parents' backyard. To complicate things further, we were planting a church in the Philippines at the same time.

I am not a great believer in dwelling on the past, but I know that I built some great qualities and habits into my life, not so much by choice but rather by necessity, at this time. One major lesson I learned was to value that which God has given you, a partner for life. Another lesson is that facts are facts, but God's truths are more valuable and more powerful.

Dean and I had seen many miracles happen in the developing countries in which we traveled before our crises, but I saw the supernatural work at a new level through our marriage.

Did God wave a wand and supernaturally make us love one another again amidst the mess? How I spent day after day hoping this would happen. But no, it was more through prayer, hard work, and forgiveness - learning to hold one's nasty tongue and to change.

And so today I am a true believer that miracles happen, and that God is a God of the supernatural if we will allow it in our lives. We don't spend our time praying that the other will change, but that we ourselves are open to change.

When crises hit, it is wise to cope with the day but always look ahead to a better future. If we look only at the day, it can be depressing if we see no change, only the dreariness of pain. As I looked at Dean, or no Dean (he had moved out), each day, I saw only a man that was causing me pain. A better vision was to see myself getting better, what I could do to love the children or what study I could commence as a mom. It is very difficult to try to look through a fog of hurt and despair, but God honors our steps of faith and our efforts.

Obviously our marriage reconciled, but this does not happen for all. I prayed, fasted, cried (not always out to God), screamed, phoned great friends (not always at the best of hours,) and meditated on Scripture. I pasted scriptures and passages on my bedroom wall so that when I woke in the morning it was the first thing that I saw. My asset was that despite pain and disillusion, I stayed in church and continued to believe in a loving and faithful God.

This does not necessarily determine that God will restore every marriage, but He restores the person and brings them into victory within themselves.

Our lives are not about ourselves so much as it is about others. This is always tough to take hold of, as most of us want the world to revolve around our wants and needs. The thing is though, when we live in this self-obsessed state we are not good company. When we spend our time giving to others, we experience a type of happiness not found when serving only our own needs. In our case, we had two very young sons that needed to be loved and raised despite our mess.

I felt a great responsibility to my children that if I was going to set them up for a successful life, I wanted to provide them with great examples. Proverbs 13:22 says,

> **22*A good man leaves an inheritance to his children's children, But the wealth of the sinner is stored up for the righteous.***

To me, to leave them with great memories of their parent's marriage and their family life was very important. I realized that a lot of the way they would live and relate would be modeled from their own upbringing.

Why was it necessary to stay faithful to God? Because I knew that God was with me, and in my future, and so to stay locked into the past and into the pain of the present was detrimental to my future. I already knew that I was paying the consequences of the bad habits of my past in that present day.

Did I think that my situation was fair? No. But these thoughts are a waste of time and lead to only a life full of depression and bitterness. And so I compiled the following points and keys as some suggestions that helped me cope, change, and build a new life. They will not all apply to everyone, but then again, we are all so different. Pick and choose at your own discretion.

. . . .

Jeremiah 29:11-12 says, *"For I know the thoughts that I think toward you, says the LORD, thoughts of peace and not of evil, to give you a future and a hope."* As previously stated, I found various scriptures that comforted me and gave me a vision for change and my future. The above scripture was and still is one of my favorites. And so I read and meditated on it each day until I found the scriptures, rather than my own depressing situation, preoccupied my mind.

Replenish yourself with God regularly through prayer, reading, and worship. Avoid too much melancholy music that makes one sad! And make sure that you see Him as a close and loving Father rather than removed and distant.

Keep great Godly friendships around you. Be in church as often as you are able, even though you may not feel that everyone there is supportive of your situation. It is vital to listen to advice.

Realize that God (Truth) is bigger than the crisis (fact). Your career may have collapsed, but God is bigger than a career. Your marriage may have ended, but you are more than a husband or wife, and God loves you no matter what. Develop other areas of your life knowing that God is a really big and good God.

Allow yourself to feel pain. Allow yourself to cry or voice it in a safe arena.

Watch your expectations of others. We need their support,

but those around us need to continue to maintain their own responsibilities. Even during our pain we need to realize and understand this.

Reevaluate your priorities and set this new pattern up in your life.

Looking for change in daily circumstances is depressing. Rather look beyond this, keep busy, and keep your goals before you.

Listen to and take the advice of your leaders. Some of it is difficult to hear but it is wisdom for life. Proverbs 19:20 says, **"Listen to counsel and receive instruction, That you may be wise in your latter days."**

Sources

Chapter 1
22: *"doers of the Word"*: James 1:22.
23: *"doers of the Word"*: James 1:22.
23: *"Church is just like..."*: Ephesians 5:22-33.

Chapter 2
25: *Hybels*: Bill Hybels, *Courageous Leadership*. Grand Rapids, Michigan: Zondervan, 2002.

Chapter 3
34: *"put on love"*: Colossians 3:14

Chapter 5
41: *"In a good..."*: Pastor Peter McHugh, *Fiance's Guide: How to Have a Successful Marriage*. Sydney, Australia: CCC Oxford Falls.
42: *"There are different..."*: H. Norman Wright and Wes Roberts, *Before You Say I Do: A Marriage Preparation Manual for Couples*. Eugene, Oregon: Harvest House, 1977.
44-46: *Scripture choices and titles:* H. Norman Wright and Wes Roberts, *Before You Say I Do: A Marriage Preparation Manual for Couples*. Eugene, Oregon: Harvest House, 1977.

Chapter 7
61: *Fairfield:* James Fairfield, *When You Don't Agree*. Scottsdale, Arizona: Herald Press, 1977.
62: *"Instead of..."*: H. Norman Wright and Wes Roberts, *Before You Say I Do: A Marriage Preparation Manual for Couples*. Eugene, Oregon: Harvest House, 1977.

Chapter 11

84: *"These statements..."*: H. Norman Wright and Wes Roberts, *Before You Say I Do: A Marriage Preparation Manual for Couples*. Eugene, Oregon: Harvest House, 1977.

85: *"Despite it sounding..."*: Pastor Peter McHugh, *Fiance's Guide: How to Have a Successful Marriage*. Sydney, Australia: CCC Oxford Falls.

91: *"Choice of church..."*: H. Norman Wright and Wes Roberts, *Before You Say I Do: A Marriage Preparation Manual for Couples*. Eugene, Oregon: Harvest House, 1977.

Chapter 12

97: *"Budgeting suggestions..."*: H. Norman Wright and Wes Roberts, *Before You Say I Do: A Marriage Preparation Manual for Couples*. Eugene, Oregon: Harvest House, 1977.

Special Acknowledgement

I would like to express gratitude to Senior Minister Peter McHugh for the impact that his guidance in the area of marriage has had on my life and my marriage. Many of the ideas and concepts that he taught have become integrated into my understanding of relationships and marriage and therefore can be found woven throughout this book.

About The Author

Dean and Jill Sweetman are senior pastors of Christian City Church Atlanta in Lawrenceville, Georgia. They, with their two children, Barnabas and Jacob, were sent out from Australia in 1996 to commence the great work of birthing a church.

They are part of the movement, Christian City Church International, that began in 1980 in Sydney, Australia under Dr. Phil Pringle. Presently in the movement there are more than 130 churches around the world, 24 in North America.

Dean and Jill married in 1985. Dean was a youth pastor at the time while Jill was a schoolteacher. While Dean moved extensively into third world traveling and birthing churches and holding evangelistic crusades, Jill invested her time in the planting of a Christian school through their church, CCC Oxford Falls in Sydney.

Through the years, God placed a desire in their hearts to plant a church in Atlanta. Today CCC Atlanta has a thriving congregation of more than 1500 members. CCC Atlanta is committed to winning the lost, making disciples and empowering the saints.